HANNAH AND HER SISTERS

HANNAH AND HER SISTERS

WOODY ALLEN

VINTAGE BOOKS
A DIVISION OF
RANDOM HOUSE
NEW YORK

A Vintage Original, January 1987
First Edition

Photographs by Brian Hamill/ Photoreporters

*The italicized passages that describe the action
have been provided by the publisher.*

Library of Congress Cataloging-in-Publication Data
Allen, Woody.
Hannah and her sisters.
I. Title.
PN1997.H2584 1987   791.43'72   86-40153
ISBN 0-394-74749-6 (pbk.)

Manufactured in the United States of America
10 9 8 7 6 5 4 3 2 1

HANNAH AND HER SISTERS

Orion Pictures

An ORION® Pictures Release

The Orion logo, with its background of celestial stars, appears on the screen as "You Made Me Love You" begins to play in sultry 1940s style. White credits pop on and off a black screen:

A JACK ROLLINS AND CHARLES H. JOFFE PRODUCTION

HANNAH AND HER SISTERS

CAST
(in alphabetical order)

Woody Allen	*Lloyd Nolan*
Michael Caine	*Maureen O'Sullivan*
Mia Farrow	*Daniel Stern*
Carrie Fisher	*Max Von Sydow*
Barbara Hershey	*Dianne Wiest*

CASTING
JULIET TAYLOR

EDITOR
SUSAN E. MORSE, A.C.E.

COSTUME DESIGNER
JEFFREY KURLAND

PRODUCTION DESIGNER
STUART WURTZEL

WOODY ALLEN

DIRECTOR OF PHOTOGRAPHY
CARLO DI PALMA, A.I.C.

EXECUTIVE PRODUCERS
JACK ROLLINS
CHARLES H. JOFFE

PRODUCED BY
ROBERT GREENHUT

WRITTEN AND DIRECTED BY
WOODY ALLEN

As the last credit appears, the song ends in a crescendo and the screen fades to total black.

Immediately, a new melody begins, an uptempo jazz number, as a title appears on the screen.

God, she's beautiful...

CUT TO:
INTERIOR. HANNAH'S APARTMENT—NIGHT.

A full face of Lee, wearing a gray sweater and leaning against the dining room doorway. She gazes into the camera with a half-smile on her face as Elliot speaks over the screen.

ELLIOT'S VOICE-OVER   God, she's beautiful.
Lee glances over her shoulder, then turns from the doorway and walks away. The camera follows her, moving across a book- and photograph-filled bookshelf that obscures her from view as she walks into a crowded, comfortable vestibule. People, some holding drinks, some just entering the apartment, surround her. Everyone is talking at once, carrying on easy, familiar conversation.

ELLIOT'S VOICE-OVER   She's got the prettiest eyes, and she looks so sexy in that sweater.

Lee smiles at the various people, exchanging greetings.

LEE   Hi, how are you?
Two more guests enter the apartment; the vestibule is full now. Still walking, Lee lightly hugs one of the children as she continues on her way towards the living room. Elliot's voice, as well as the jazzy music, is heard.

ELLIOT'S VOICE-OVER   I just want to be alone with her and hold her and kiss her . . .
Lee walks into the living room, turning her head back for a moment to talk to the child she has just hugged.

ELLIOT'S VOICE-OVER   . . . and tell her how much I love her and take care of her. Stop it, you idiot. She's your wife's sister. But I can't help it.
The camera is still moving with Lee as she smiles and stops to chat with her mother. Elliot's voice, as well as the music, continues over the low din of warm conversation.

ELLIOT'S VOICE-OVER   I'm consumed by her. It's been months now. I dream about her. I-I, I think about her at the office. Oh, Lee. (Sighing) What am I gonna do?
Lee starts to walk off again, finishing her conversation with her mother. She passes several other guests, then turns to greet April, giving her a warm, brief hug.

ELLIOT'S VOICE-OVER   I hear myself mooning over you, and it's disgusting. Before, when she . . .
Elliot's voice-over continues as he is actually seen, standing in a doorway having a conversation with a gesturing, rotund man. Both are holding drinks as Lee, carrying a tray of hors d'oeuvres and two drinks, walks between them. The space is very tight; the men hold up their drinks to make room for her.

ELLIOT'S VOICE-OVER   . . . squeezed past me in the doorway, and I smelled that perfume on the back of her neck . . .
Elliot watches Lee walk off; the other man, oblivious, continues to

talk. *Elliot reluctantly returns to the conversation, but he can't help turning his head to gaze at the offscreen Lee as the other man chatters on.*

ELLIOT'S VOICE-OVER . . . Jesus, I, I thought I was gonna swoon! Easy . . .
The camera resumes following a smiling Lee. She has just put down the tray and drinks near April, and briskly and obliviously, she walks past a doorway where Elliot, still ruminating, watches her, entranced.

ELLIOT'S VOICE-OVER You're a dignified financial advisor. It doesn't look good for you to swoon.
The camera stays with Elliot, who is still watching the offscreen Lee. In the background, guests continue to chatter warmly with each other. Hannah, carrying a tray of hors d'oeuvres, walks up behind the distracted Elliot.

HANNAH *(Nibbling on an hors d'oeuvre)* Elliot? Elliot? *(Rubbing his shoulder)* Sweetheart?
Elliot returns from his reveries with a start.

ELLIOT *(Turning to Hannah)* Mm-hm?

HANNAH *(Pointing to the tray)* Have you tried these? These are wonderful. *(Nibbling, swallowing)* Holly and her friend made them.
Elliot, taking one of the hors d'oeuvres, starts nibbling as well as he and Hannah walk past the bookshelf into the living room.

ELLIOT *(Swallowing)* They're fantastic.

HANNAH *(Overlapping, still eating)* Aren't they great?

ELLIOT Your sister is an unbelievable cook.

HANNAH *(Swallowing)* I know! I know!
Elliot and Hannah, eating and talking, walk past a hallway and offscreen as Holly appears, walking down the hallway. She holds a drink and a plate of hors d'oeuvres; she stands at the entrance to the hallway, eating and looking at the offscreen guests.

HANNAH *(Walking offscreen)* She has all the cooking talent.

ELLIOT *(Walking offscreen swallowing)* No, she doesn't, either. You've got tons as well.

HANNAH *(Offscreen)* Ohhh, but I've eaten five of these.
Holly, standing in the hallway onscreen, swallows loudly.

ELLIOT *(Offscreen, overlapping Holly)* Holly, why don't you open your own restaurant?

HOLLY *(Turning to the offscreen Elliot and Hannah, trying to swallow)* Mmm, we practically are. Well . . . *(Holding her hand to her mouth)* not a restaurant, but . . . *(Swallowing)* April and I are going to do some catering!

HANNAH *(Offscreen)* What? You're kidding!

HOLLY *(Nodding)* No, no, we decided!
Holly takes a sip of her drink as Hannah and Elliot walk over to her.

HANNAH Perfect!

HOLLY *(Nodding and swallowing)* Mmm . . . I mean, we love to cook for our friends, so *(Gesturing)* we thought until an acting job comes through, we could just make some extra money, you know, doing a few private parties.

ELLIOT *(Nodding)* Great idea.

HANNAH *(Agreeing)* I know.

ELLIOT *(Overlapping Hannah)* That's where your talent lies.

HOLLY *(Swallowing and nodding)* I know.
  Holly and Hannah begin to laugh.

HOLLY *(Gesturing to Elliot, still laughing)* Get outta here. *(To Hannah)* Could I speak to you privately?

HANNAH Oh, sure.
  Holly and Hannah walk off; Elliot watches them leave.

ELLIOT *(Calling after them as he nibbles on an hors d'oeuvre)* I'm her husband! She tells me anything!

CUT TO:
INTERIOR. HANNAH'S KITCHEN—NIGHT.

Hannah, licking her fingers, walks past a memo-cluttered refrigerator to the stove as Holly, behind her, begins to speak. The faint sounds of music are still heard.

HOLLY Hannah, I have to borrow some more money. *(Sipping her drink)* Don't get upset.

HANNAH *(Stirring some food in a saucepan on the stove)* Mmm, I never get upset over that. Mmm?

HOLLY This is the last time, I promise. And I'm keeping strict accounts.

As Holly talks, sipping her drink, Hannah busily works in the kitchen, which contains a large center table stacked with bowls and plates of food, hanging pots and pans, and general party clutter. She walks on- and offscreen as she talks and listens to her sister.

HANNAH   Holly, please. Don't insult me.

HOLLY *(Putting her empty glass and plate down on the table)* Someday, I'll pay it all back.

HANNAH   I know. H-how much do you need?

HOLLY   Two thousand dollars.
Hannah, who'd been mashing some food in a bowl on a nearby counter, hesitates momentarily. She turns to Holly.

HANNAH *(Trying to nod her head casually)*   Uh-huh.

HOLLY *(Gesturing, her back to the camera)*   Hannah, I know it's a lot, but my friend April and I, we have this catering idea I think's going to be great.
Hannah, licking her fingers, walks past Holly.

HOLLY *(Turning to face Hannah)*   You admit that we're great cooks, right?

HANNAH *(Nodding, back at the stove now, stirring in a pot)*   Yeah.

HOLLY *(Putting her hands in her pockets)*   Well, in order to get started, there's just a few things I have to buy . . . *(Gesturing)* and some old debts I have outstanding.

HANNAH *(Looking at her sister)*   Will you just tell me one thing?

HOLLY *(Nodding)*   Okay.

HANNAH   Are we talking about cocaine again?

HOLLY *(Shaking her head no)*   I swear. I swear. We've already got some requests to do a few dinner parties.

A timer goes off. Hannah walks past Holly to attend to some food on a different stove. Holly turns to face her. Only Holly is seen as she talks to the offscreen Hannah, the camera moving in closer on her face. As Holly speaks, she distractedly nibbles an hors d'oeuvre. In the background, her parents can be heard singing in the living room.

HOLLY   I mean, obviously, I'm not going to be a caterer forever, you know. We both still go to auditions. Something could turn up at any moment. But the parties are at night, days are free, I can still take my acting class. I haven't done drugs in a year.
Holly pops another hors d'oeuvre into her mouth as the background singing gets louder and the film cuts to:

INTERIOR. HANNAH'S LIVING ROOM—NIGHT.

The living room is crowded with family and guests sitting comfortably on chairs near the piano, where Evan, Hannah's father, plays "Bewitched" as Hannah's mother, Norma, sits nearby, accompanying him in their duet. A child is sprawled out under a blanket on a sofa; some guests chatter quietly; others drink and eat, listening.

EVAN AND NORMA *(Singing)*   "A whimpering, simpering / Child again / Bewitched, bothered, and bewildered / Am I . . ."
As they continue to sing, the film cuts back to the kitchen, where Lee, carrying some glasses, enters through the doorway.

LEE   Mom and Dad are floating down memory lane again!
Lee walks over to her sisters, putting the glasses down on a counter. Hannah is scooping seeds out of a cantaloupe at the sink. Holly, leaning on the table, sips her drink. The music from the living room is softly heard as the three sisters chat comfortably and easily with each other.

HANNAH *(Smiling and turning to Lee)*   Aah . . . Hey, have you tried Holly and her friend's shrimp puffs?

LEE *(Nodding to Holly, touching her arm)* I think they're fantastic.

HANNAH *(To Holly)* You've outdone yourself.

HOLLY *(Overlapping her sisters, shrugging and smiling)* Oh, my God. Thank you.

LEE *(Interrupting, to Hannah)* I need an antihistamine. Mom thinks she's feeling her asthma, and so . . .

HANNAH *(Overlapping)* Ohh?

HOLLY *(Overlapping, lighting a cigarette)* Uh-oh.

LEE *(Continuing)* . . . before she starts turning into Camille . . . *(Laughing)*

HOLLY *(Overlapping)* Yeah, Mom's Camille when she gets up in the morning.

LEE *(Turning to Holly)* At least she isn't drinking. Did you notice?

HOLLY *(Nodding)* Mm-hm.

HANNAH *(Turning to look at her sisters, laughing)* Doesn't she look great in that new dress?

HOLLY *(Nodding)* Yeah.

LEE *(Nodding)* Yeah.
The sisters all talk at once; Hannah is still working at the sink.

HANNAH Don't you think she does?

HOLLY She really does, though.

LEE *(Turning towards the sink)* Yeah, she knows it, too, 'cause she's flirting with all the men here.

HOLLY *(Puffing on her cigarette)* God.

HANNAH *(Scooping out some cantaloupe seeds)* Maybe when she's eighty, she'll stop straightening her garter belt when there's a guy around.

HOLLY *(To Lee, laughing)* I should get a garter belt.

LEE *(Laughing)* Yeah.

HOLLY *(Looking down at herself)* Get a garter belt . . . *(Sipping her drink)* Get a garter belt and flirt.

LEE *(Laughing, to Hannah)* Where are the antihistamines?

HANNAH Oh, I don— Ask Elliot for that. Uh, he's got them somewhere.

LEE *(Nodding)* Okay.
Lee leaves the kitchen. Holly, puffing on her cigarette, watches her go.

HOLLY *(Sighing)* Frederick didn't come with her.

HANNAH *(Turning to Holly, still working at the sink)* When does Frederick ever come with her?

HOLLY *(Whispering intently)* Tch. He's such an angry . . . he's such a depressive. I thought she was moving out!
Hannah shakes her head in disapproval while Holly angrily takes another sip of her drink.

And the film cuts briefly back to the living room, where Evan is still playing the piano and singing. The camera moves past him and a few guests to Norma, who is enthusiastically singing along, looking at Evan and moving her hands.

EVAN AND NORMA *(Singing)* "A pill he is / But still he is / All mine and I'll / Keep him until he is / Bewitched, a'both—"

CUT TO:
INTERIOR. HANNAH'S DINING ROOM—NIGHT.

The table is beautifully set for Thanksgiving dinner, complete with candles, flowers, cut crystal, china, and silver. Hannah's children are playing in the room as Hannah enters, carrying a huge roast turkey. Behind her is Holly, carrying a casserole. Hannah's parents can still be heard singing in the background.

HANNAH *(To the children)* Watch out, you guys. Beep-beep!

HOLLY *(Overlapping)* Oh, your kids are so adorable.

CHILDREN *(Walking through the doorway)* Bye! Bye!

HOLLY *(Putting down her bowl on the table)* God, it gets so lonely on the holidays.

HANNAH *(Setting down the turkey on the opposite end of the table)* Oh, gosh. Well, you know, that's why I invited Phil Gammage tonight.
As the sisters talk, the piano music stops. There's the sound of light applause as Evan begins a new song, faintly heard in the dining room.

HOLLY *(Grimacing, reacting to Hannah)*   Oh, Hannah!

HANNAH *(Overlapping)*   It's, uh, you never know—

HOLLY *(Interrupting, gesturing)*   He's such a loser!

HANNAH   He's not a loser at all!

HOLLY *(Shaking her head)*   Oh, he's such a loser!

HANNAH *(Overlapping, lighting a set of candles on the table)*   He's the headmaster of Daisy's school.

HOLLY   Oh, perfect! He reminds me of Ichabod Crane. *(Moving her hand up and down her throat)* His Adam's apple keeps jumping up and down whenever he gets excited.

HANNAH *(Laughing)*   Listen. He's a lot better than your ex-husband. He's got a good job. *(Handing a pack of matches to Holly)* Would you light those, please? He's-he's-he's not a dope addict or anything.

HOLLY *(Striking a match to light another set of candles).*   Give me a break.

APRIL *(Offscreen)*   Am I interrupting . . .
The film cuts to April, standing in the doorway of the dining room and holding a drink.

APRIL *(Continuing)*   . . . any sister talk?

HANNAH *(Offscreen)*   Mm-mm!

HOLLY *(Offscreen)*   Come in.
The camera moves with April as she walks over to the table, where Hannah and Holly are lighting candles.

APRIL   Oh, good . . .

HANNAH   *(Overlapping, still offscreen)*   Come in, come in.

APRIL *(Gesturing)* . . . because there are no interesting single men at this party!

HANNAH *(Now onscreen)* Oh, listen . . .

HOLLY *(Interrupting, waving out her match)* I know. It's terrible!

APRIL *(Shaking her head)* I mean, I've looked everywhere.

HANNAH *(Picking at the turkey and gesturing)* Maybe April would like Phil. Phil Gammage, the tall guy in there by the piano.
Holly groans, looking at her sister, while April sips her drink and nods.

APRIL *(Pointing to herself)* Hm-mm. Oh, yeah. I met Phil.

HANNAH *(Looking at April, nodding)* Mmm?

APRIL He's the— He looks like Ichabod Crane?
Hannah screams with laughter as she walks toward the end of the table, past a gleeful Holly, who points her finger at Hannah as she passes. Hannah, still laughing, playfully pushes the accusing finger away.

APRIL *(Laughing with the sisters, gesturing)* I love that. That's my type.

HANNAH *(Shaking her head, laughing)* I can't believe it!
She walks over to a nearby china cabinet.

APRIL *(Nodding and looking at Hannah)* No, really, I really like him a lot.

HOLLY *(Overlapping, laughing and gesturing)* No, really, we mustn't get discouraged.
As Holly continues to tease her sister, Hannah opens a drawer in the cabinet. She takes out two apples decorated with paper turkey heads and tails and hands them to April.

HOLLY *(Fussing at the table)* Hannah will invite some men over who don't look like Ichabod Crane.

APRIL *(Overlapping)* Mmm.
  April starts to put the turkey apples on the table. A bemused Hannah takes two more out of the cabinet and places one of them on the table as well.

HOLLY *(Straightening a table setting)* Not this Thanksgiving, you know.

HANNAH *(Overlapping, to April, who has just set down her apples)* Here. Be careful with those.

HOLLY *(Continuing her teasing, gesturing)* Maybe at Christmas, New Year's. If not this New Year's, maybe next New Year's. *While Holly is talking, Hannah hands her the last turkey apple, accidentally sticking her with one of the toothpicks that keeps the decorations in place.*

HOLLY *(Reacting)* Ouch!

HANNAH *(Turning to her sister in surprise)* Oh!
  The film cuts to a short hallway leading to a bathroom in Hannah's apartment. In the foreground is a standing lamp. In the background, Elliot is seen walking inside the bathroom, looking around the room. Light piano music is dimly heard.

ELLIOT *(Searching)* Must be here someplace.
  He walks out of the bathroom, moving down the hallway towards the camera.

LEE *(Offscreen)* Oh, you know, I, I love that book you lent me. *The Easter Parade?* You were right. It had very special meaning for me.

ELLIOT How's Frederick? He didn't come.
  Elliot walks into the bedroom as Lee continues to talk offscreen. The

camera, leaving Elliot, moves across the room, past a wall of framed paintings, a headboard and bed, a night table and lamp, revealing Lee. She is flipping through a book by a curtained window.

LEE *(Offscreen)* Oh, well, you know Frederick. One of his moods. Although it wasn't a bad week. He *(Onscreen)* uh, sold a picture.

ELLIOT *(Offscreen)* Oh, great.
The camera stays with Lee as she walks around the room, past another curtained window, a television set, and a rolltop desk. She absently flips through the book as she talks to the offscreen Elliot.

LEE Yeah, it was, it was one of his better drawings, a very beautiful nude study. Actually, it was of me. *(Laughing)* It's funny, you know, it's a funny feeling to know you're being hung naked in some stranger's living room.
Lee puts the book she's been holding down on the desk, only to pick up another one. She looks at the offscreen Elliot.

LEE Well, you can't tell it's me, although— *(Pausing)* You're turning all red, Elliot.
She reacts. The camera moves to a blushing Elliot, following him now as he walks across the room.

ELLIOT *(Laughing self-consciously)* Really? So, so, what else? Wh- what are you up to?

LEE *(Offscreen)* Oh, I don't know. My unemployment checks are running out. Um, I was thinking of taking some courses at Columbia with the last of my savings.
As Lee speaks, Elliot parts a hanging curtain against the wall to reveal a stereo and some records. He looks at the offscreen Lee.

ELLIOT Like, uh . . . ?

LEE *(Offscreen)* I don't know exactly.
As Elliot reaches inside the stereo shelf, grabbing a bottle of antihista-

mines, the camera moves back to Lee, who sits down on the bed. She is still holding a book.

LEE   Um, sociology, psychology maybe. I always thought I might like to work with children.
Elliot walks over to Lee; he sits down on a footstool in front of her.

ELLIOT   *(Gesturing with the bottle of pills gripped in his hand)*   Incidentally, I-I always have clients who are furnishing places. Some of them might-might be interested in buying art. Shall I, shall I call you? *(Chuckling self-consciously)*

LEE   Yeah, sure. *(Taking the bottle of pills Elliot hands her)* You know, uh, Frederick would really be grateful for a sale.
She chuckles; Elliot smiles and chuckles with her.

HANNAH *(Offscreen)*   Hey, you guys?
Elliot turns in the direction of his wife's voice.

HANNAH *(Offscreen)*   Dinner's ready.
Hannah, eating a carrot stick, enters the bedroom. The camera stays with her momentarily as she walks towards Elliot and Lee.

LEE *(Offscreen)*   Oh, great.

HANNAH *(Overlapping)*   You look so beautiful.

LEE *(Offscreen)*   Come on.

HANNAH *(Standing by Elliot and Lee)*   Doesn't she look pretty?

LEE   I bumped into your . . .

ELLIOT *(Overlapping, agreeing with Hannah)*   Yeah.

LEE *(Continuing)*   . . . ex-husband on the street the other day.

HANNAH *(Biting her carrot)*   Oh, yeah?

LEE *(Gesturing)*   He was, he's just as crazy as ever. He was on his way to get a blood test. *(Laughing, Elliot joining in.)*

HANNAH *(Reacting)* God, Mickey's such a hypochondriac. I wonder how he'd handle it if there was ever anything really wrong with him?

ELLIOT *(Standing up)* Let's go have dinner, shall we?

HANNAH *(Overlapping)* Mmm.

LEE *(Standing up, overlapping)* Good idea.

CUT TO:
INTERIOR. DINING ROOM—NIGHT.

Everyone is seated around the table for Thanksgiving dinner. Facing the camera are Holly, Lee, Norma, and Hannah. She sits to the left of Elliot, who's at the head of the table. On his right is Evan; April sits next to him. She and the other guests sit with their backs to the screen. The table overflows with food, floral decorations, and candles. In the background, the children sit at a separate table; a maid serves them turkey. The guests chatter comfortably among themselves as they eat.

EVAN *(Clanking a piece of silverware against his water glass)* Now, ladies and gentlemen . . .

HOLLY *(Making a face)* Dad.
Evan continues to clank his glass to get everyone's attention.

HOLLY Dad . . .

LEE *(Reacting, to Holly)* Oh . . .

HOLLY Dad!

EVAN *(Still clanking)* No, now . . .

HOLLY I'm starving!
Resigned, Holly puts down her silverware. Lee smothers a laugh. Norma, reacting, glances at Holly and Lee. Everyone knows what's coming.

EVAN (*Clanking away*) . . . this is a toast! This is a toast.

HANNAH (*Reaching across the table for Evan's wine glass, laughing*) Get his wine away.

EVAN This is a toast. You know this beautiful Thanksgiving dinner was all . . .
Holly laughs. Lee glances over to her, reacting. Hannah, embarrassed, reacts and sits with her hands on her face. Lee and the rest of the guests put down their silverware. They look at Evan, listening.

EVAN . . . prepared . . . by Hannah.
Hannah, embarrassed, makes a victory sign.

HANNAH (*Modestly pointing to the maid*) Uh, and a little help . . .
Lee and Holly try to suppress their laughter. Norma glares at them.

NORMA (*To her daughters*) Hey!

HANNAH (*Continuing*) . . . from Mavis, also.
Elliot wraps his arm around Hannah; he pulls her towards him affectionately and kisses her on the cheek. She hugs him back.

ELLIOT (*Hugging Hannah*) You bet.

HANNAH (*Overlapping, looking down the table while still in Elliot's embrace*) Holly and April, thanks for helping.
Mavis the maid exits, carrying some trays, as the group starts to cheer and applaud. Holly waves her napkin at April, then holds up her wine glass.

EVAN (*Overlapping the noise*) No, you did it.

HOLLY (*Overlapping, toasting her friend*) April, April!

HANNAH (*Overlapping, gesturing*) I am . . . I did slave all day.

EVAN (*Overlapping, holding out his wine glass*) And we drink to her, and we all congratulate her on her wonderful accomplishment during this last year . . . her great success in *A Doll's House*!

The group continues to cheer as they all toast Hannah. She reacts, smiling but embarrassed.

NORMA *(Overlapping, laughing)* Ya-a-a-a-y! *(Laughing)* I played Nora. I hate to tell you what year . . .

The guests, sipping their wine, quiet down as Norma continues to speak. Lee and Holly unsuccessfully try to contain their laughter. Mavis reenters the dining room to serve more food to the children.

NORMA *(Continuing)* And it's very difficult to behave like Torvald's little chipmunk without making a perfect ass out of yourself! *(Pausing while the guests laugh heartily)* Now I think that Ibsen would have been damn proud of our Hannah!

Norma toasts her daughter; everyone follows her. The applause and cheers begin anew. Hannah, reacting, chuckles.

APRIL *(Overlapping the applause and clapping loudly)* Speech! Speech! Speech!

NORMA *(Overlapping)* Yea-a-a-a-ah!

A few guests sip their wine. They all quiet down as Hannah starts her speech, glancing around the table and gesturing.

HANNAH *(Reacting)* I don't know about that. Oh, no, I just, see, I-I've been very, very lucky. W-when I had the kids, I decided to stop working and just, you know, devote myself to having the family, and I've been very, very happy *(Banging her fists lightly on the table)* but . . . I've always secretly hoped that maybe some little gem would come along and tempt me back on the stage . . .

EVAN *(Nodding)* Yeah.

HANNAH *(Overlapping)* . . . just for a second. So, now I got that out of my system and I can go back to the thing that makes me happiest.

Hannah tenderly takes Elliot's hand as she looks around the table. He, in turn, kneads her shoulder, chuckling with equal tenderness.

EVAN *(Chuckling)*   Oh, bravo! Bravo!
Hannah, still embarrassed, looks down at a plate. The group applauds once more, toasting and drinking, and warmly sounding their approval.

CUT TO:

We all had a terrific time.

Classical string music plays as the film cuts to:

EXTERIOR. MANHATTAN STREET—NIGHT.

A taxi moves down Broadway towards the camera, passing a truck on the right, the Winter Garden marquee advertising Cats, *and several buildings, and as the taxi moves offscreen, the classical music still playing, the movie cuts to the taxi's backseat. Lee sits by the window, leaning her head in her hand, a reflective look on her face. Her voice is heard over the screen.*

LEE'S VOICE-OVER   Is it my imagination, or does Elliot have a little crush on me? *(Chuckling slightly)* It's funny. I've had that thought before. He pays a lot of attention to me all the time, and he blushed tonight when we were alone in the bedroom. I wonder if he and Hannah are happy? It's funny, I . . . I still feel a little buzz from his flirting.

CUT TO:
INTERIOR. FREDERICK'S LOFT—NIGHT.

Lee stirs a cup of coffee on the counter of the loft's modern kitchen area; a nearby vase holds flowers. She walks across the loft, with its high ceilings and beige walls, holding her coffee.

LEE *(To an offscreen Frederick)*   Want some coffee or tea?

FREDERICK *(Offscreen)*   No, thank you.
Lee continues to walk, past a modern chaise, a bookcase, some sofas, two columns. Lamps hang down from the ceiling. The classical music still plays in the background. Lee stops at a plastic-enclosed work area. Frederick can be seen working at a drawing board on the other side of the clear plastic screen.

LEE *(Stirring her coffee)*   How about something to eat?

FREDERICK   No, nothing.
The background music stops.

LEE   Are you sure?

FREDERICK   Absolutely.

LEE *(Walking around the screen to Frederick)*   Mmm, what am I gonna do with you? *(Laughing)*

As Lee walks over to the drawing board where Frederick is sitting, he is seen intently cleaning some paintbrushes with a rag. Lee stands by him, leaning over the board, and looks directly at him. The table is filled with cans of brushes and artist's equipment.

LEE   God! *(Sniffing)* And why didn't you come tonight? We all had a terrific time. I really think you would have enjoyed yourself.

FREDERICK *(Not looking at Lee)*   I'm going through a period of my life where I just can't be around people. *(Putting down the brushes and wiping his hands with the same rag)* I didn't want to wind up abusing anyone.

LEE   You're not going to abuse them. They're all so sweet.

FREDERICK *(Taking off his glasses)*   Lee . . . *(Pausing, reaching for Lee's hand)* you are the only person I can be with . . . who I really look forward to being with. *(Pulling Lee to him, around the board)*

LEE *(Compliantly)*   You're too harsh with everyone. You know that, don't you?
Frederick and Lee embrace; Lee sighs.

FREDERICK *(Looking into Lee's eyes)*   Isn't it enough that I can love you?

LEE *(Sighing)*   Mmm . . .

FREDERICK   Hmm?

LEE *(Overlapping)*   . . . you're such a puzzle. *(Chuckling)* So sweet with me and so . . . contemptuous of everyone else. *(Sighing)*

FREDERICK *(Sniffing)*   Well, there was a time *(Sniffing again)* when you were very happy to be only with me. You wanted to learn everything about poetry, about music.

LEE *(Nodding)* Mm-hm.

FREDERICK Have I really taught you everything I have to give?
(Shaking his head) I don't think so.
Lee kisses Frederick twice, then releases him and walks out of the work area.

LEE *(Turning her head in Frederick's direction)* Oh, Elliot said he might have a couple of clients for you.
Lee walks over to the loft's stereo area, pulling up the sleeves of her sweater as Frederick talks.

FREDERICK *(Offscreen)* I'm sure all those morons he handles have a deep feeling for art.
Lee picks up a book from the stereo shelf. She leans back against the unit, glancing through its pages.

LEE *(Flipping through the book)* Mmm *(Chuckling)* you never know. They might. He's just trying to do the nice thing.

FREDERICK *(Offscreen)* Because he likes you.

LEE *(Looking up from the book)* Me?

FREDERICK Yeah.
Frederick, leaving his work area, walks past Lee; his hands are in his pockets.

FREDERICK *(Looking at Lee as he goes by)* Elliot lusts after you.

LEE Based on what? You never even see him.
The camera stays with Frederick as he walks into the loft's bedroom area.

FREDERICK Based on . . . whenever you see him, you always come home full of books he's recommended . . .
He sits down at the foot of the bed and starts taking off his shoes.

FREDERICK *(Continuing)* . . . or films you must see or . . . *(Shrugging)*

LEE *(Walking over to him)* Oh, no, no, no. He's my sister's husband. And I think if you gave him half a chance, you'd like him. He's very intelligent.
Lee sits down next to Frederick; he takes her hand.

FREDERICK He's a glorified accountant, and he's after you. *(Kissing Lee's hand)* And I prefer to sell my work to people who appreciate it, not to rock stars. *(Kissing Lee's face)* You understand?
Lee kisses Frederick back on the cheek. They embrace. Frederick laughs; their embrace gets tighter.

LEE *(Sighing)* Ohhh!

CUT TO:

The hypochondriac.

Upbeat jazz plays in the background and continues as the film cuts to:

INTERIOR. TV STUDIO CORRIDOR—NIGHT.

Metal elevator doors open and Mickey Sachs, a high-powered television producer, walks out, deep in conversation with his assistants, Paul and Larry. As the elevator operator begins to reclose the door with his passengers, Mickey, his assistants fast behind, walks down an office corridor past busy groups of studio personnel. Indistinct conversation, as well as the jazz, is heard in the background as the trio talk.

MICKEY *(Gesturing)*   What do you mean, they won't let us do the sketch?

PAUL   Talk to Standards and Practices. They think it's too dirty.
The trio pass Mary, another assistant, in conversation with two other co-workers. She holds a clipboard.

MICKEY   But we showed it to them in rehearsal!
Without missing a beat, he takes Mary's wrist and continues walking.

MICKEY *(To Paul)*   You know, what'd they do, figure out what the words mean?
A foursome now, they briskly walk past a man and a woman going over a script. Mary and Mickey lead; Paul and Larry follow.

MARY   Mickey, we got a half hour to air!
As the group walks through a large doorway, Larry catches up to Mickey.

LARRY   We're short! The show is five minutes short!
The group turns right into a new corridor, briefly off the screen. As they scurry off, their voices are heard.

MICKEY   How could it be short? We timed everything *(Offscreen)* long.

PAUL *(Offscreen)*   If we have to . . .

They are all now seen walking down the new corridor towards the camera. The corridor is crowded with busy TV personnel. The group continues to talk frantically as people hurry past them. One man pushes rudely past Mary as he walks; she looks back at him briefly.

PAUL *(Continuing)* . . . pull out the sketch, then we'll be ten minutes short!

MICKEY *(Gesturing)* I don't know how they can do that to us. That's— We go on in thirty minutes, right?
Mary checks her wristwatch as they rush down the corridor.

LARRY *(Squeezing past several passersby)* They're doing it because our ratings are low.

MICKEY *(Nervously rubbing his forehead)* I got such a migraine.
As the group briskly walks past an open door, Gail, another assistant, runs out, brandishing her glasses.

GAIL *(Offscreen)* Hey, Mickey!
Gail runs in front of the group. Without missing a step, she faces Mickey and walks backwards, gesturing and talking frantically.

GAIL Mickey! Listen, we better go right to Ronny's dressing room. This kid must have taken sixteen hundred Quaaludes. I don't think he's going to be able to do the show!
The fast-tracking group turns the corner. Gail pats Mickey's back; she gestures in exasperation.

MICKEY *(Gesturing towards heaven)* Why me, Lord? What did I—
He is interrupted by Ed Smythe, an official from the Standards and Practices Department, who's been standing in the corridor waiting for Mickey. Mickey stops and shakes Ed's hand as if he'd known the official would be there. Gail stops by his side while the others walk into a background studio doorway that is busy with scurrying personnel.

MICKEY You— *(Pointing)* Standards and Practices?

ED   Ed Smythe, yes.

MICKEY   Okay. Why, all of a sudden, is the sketch dirty? *(Putting his hands on his hips)*

ED *(Gesturing)*   Child molestation is a touchy subject . . .

MICKEY *(Overlapping, looking at Gail)*   Could you—

ED *(Continuing)*   . . . with the affiliates.

MICKEY *(Overlapping and grunting)*   Read the papers! Half the country's doing it!

ED *(Pointing at Mickey)*   Yes, but you name names.

MICKEY *(Gesturing)*   We nev— We don't name names! *(Turning to Gail for support, briefly touching her shoulders, then looking back at Ed)* We say the Pope.

GAIL *(Gesturing emphatically)*   We always say the Pope!

ED   That sketch . . .

MICKEY *(Overlapping)*   We—

ED *(Continuing)*   . . . cannot go on the air.
A writer, holding a script, walks out of the background studio, looking around.

MICKEY   Oh, Je—

WRITER *(Interrupting, shouting)*   Hey!
Mickey, Gail, and Ed turn towards the writer.

WRITER *(Angrily slapping his script)*   Who changed my sketch about the PLO?
Mickey and Gail walk over to the angry writer, Ed forgotten with this new crisis.

MICKEY *(Gesturing)*   I had to make some cuts. It's four lousy lines!

WRITER   The whole premise is ruined!
Mickey, Gail, and the writer start walking down a corridor adjacent to the studio.

MICKEY *(Gesturing, trying to calm the writer down)*   Oh, you're crazy! It's not so delicate. Everybody's married to every line. *The writer reacts angrily. Gail tries to get Mickey's attention as they walk.*

GAIL *(Tapping Mickey's shoulder)*   Mickey, I can—

WRITER *(Interrupting, angrily gesturing)*   I don't care! I don't want anyone tampering with my goddamn work without telling me!

MICKEY *(Shrugging)*   Okay.

WRITER *(Pointing angrily)*   You want 'em cut?! I'll cut 'em my-self!
Mickey, still in surprised shock, turns away from the angry writer. He stands by an open dressing room, where Ron, an actor, slouches, dazed, in a chair facing a makeup mirror. People mill in the background behind the actor.

MICKEY *(Shrugging, distracted)*   All right, all right. *(Muttering)*

GAIL *(Overlapping, trying to get Mickey's attention and gesturing)*   Mickey, Mickey, listen, listen.

MICKEY *(Distractedly, his mind still on the writer)*   You know . . . *(Muttering as the writer passes him and walks away)*

GAIL *(Overlapping, gesturing)*   In-in-in-instead of the child molestation sketch, why don't we repeat the Cardinal Spellman–Ronald Reagan homosexual dance number?

MICKEY *(Still distracted, looking off)* No—

RON *(Overlapping)* I don't feel good, Mickey.
Mickey, remembering Ron, runs into the dressing room. Gail follows him. Inside, a man and a woman talk, ignoring Ron. They share a drink in a paper cup. The woman looks back at Ron; she gestures with disgust.

MICKEY *(Gesturing)* Yeah, wh— Yeah, what did you do? Swallow a drugstore?!
Ron coughs.

MICKEY *(To Gail)* Look at this guy.

GAIL *(Overlapping, touching Ron's chair)* Yeah?

RON *(Groaning)* I lost my voice.
Gail walks around the chair. The camera shows she and Mickey talking to Ron through the reflection in the cluttered makeup mirror.

MICKEY *(Reacting)* Oh, Jesus!

GAIL *(Gesturing)* Ron . . . Ronny, you know you do have to go on in twenty-five minutes.
Ron sighs.

MICKEY *(Looking around, touching his stomach)* Hey, does anybody got a Tagamet? My, my ulcer's starting to kill me!

RON *(Sighing)* You want a Quaalude?
Mickey, as reflected in the mirror, starts to pace as the movie cuts to:

EXTERIOR. BEVERLY HILLS BOULEVARD—DAY.

Norman, a Los Angeles TV producer and Mickey's former partner, is driving down a peaceful street lined with palm trees. He's wearing sunglasses and headphones. He clicks his fingers in time to the music only he hears on his Walkman. He's smiling contentedly while Mickey talks over the sun-filled scene. The continuous background jazz plays louder.

MICKEY'S VOICE-OVER   Christ, this show is ruining my health! Meanwhile, my ex-partner moves to California and every stupid show he produces turns out to be a big hit. Brother, what am I gonna do with my life? Speaking of that, I-I . . . gotta remember to see my ex-wife tomorrow. 'Tch.

CUT TO:
INTERIOR. HANNAH'S APARTMENT FOYER—DAY.

As Mickey finishes his ruminations, Hannah is seen walking towards her front door. She opens it, her back to the camera. Mickey stands there holding two boxed gifts. The jazz stops.

HANNAH   Hi! Hi!

MICKEY *(Overlapping, sniffing)*   I know . . . I know.

HANNAH   Glad you could put in an appearance.

MICKEY *(Gesturing)*   I got two minutes.

HANNAH *(Overlapping)*   Very good.
Hannah nods as Mickey comes inside. She closes the door behind him.

MICKEY *(Overlapping)*   I got two minutes. 'Cause, God, the show is killing me. I got a million appointments today. It just so happens it fell this way.
Hannah continues to nod patiently, patting Mickey on the back, as they make their way aross the foyer into the den, where the twins are playing. Mickey wears his coat.

MICKEY   I gotta see new comedians later, I've gotta—

HANNAH *(Interrupting)*   Two minutes on your sons' birthday. You know, it's not going to kill you.
Her voice trails off as Mickey walks over to the twins.

MICKEY   Happy Birthday, fellas! Happy Birthday!
Hannah's twins greet Mickey with cries of "Hi, Daddy!" and indistinct chatter.

HANNAH *(Overlapping their chatter, bending down to talk to her sons)*   Guys, look what Daddy brought. Presents!
Mickey hands a gift to each twin. They grow quiet, suddenly shy.

MICKEY *(To his sons)*   Yeah, aren't you like, you know . . .

HANNAH *(Overlapping)*   Huh?

MICKEY *(Continuing, holding out his arms)*   . . . a little, uh, hey! A little hug! What is this? Now how 'bout a little action from the kids?
The twins put down their gifts, one on the sofa, one on the coffee table, and hug their father.

MICKEY *(Turning to Hannah)*   How is everything?

HANNAH *(Picking up the gift on the sofa and nodding)*   Everything's good. Everything's fine.

MICKEY *(Nodding, overlapping)*   Yeah? Yeah? *(Pointing)* Okay, kids, you can open the presents now.

HANNAH *(Overlapping)*   Here, you guys. Open them up.
Hannah makes room on the coffee table for the gift she is holding; she places it next to the other one. The boys start opening them.

MICKEY   Let me get a little reaction here. *(To Hannah, putting his hands in his pockets)* How's Elliot?

HANNAH   He's fine.

MICKEY   Yeah?

HANNAH *(Overlapping)*   Oh, you know what? I'm trying to convince him to produce a play.

MICKEY   Oh!

HANNAH   I think he'll find that satisfying.

MICKEY *(Nodding)*   Really? That'll be terrific for him, I think.

HANNAH   I think so.

MICKEY   I like him. I think he's a sweet guy.

HANNAH *(Stroking one of the twins' backs)*   Yeah.

MICKEY   The few times that I've met him . . . *(Pointing to the baseball mitt twin #1 has taken out of his box)* Isn't that a great mitt?

TWIN #1   Thank you, Daddy.

MICKEY *(Overlapping to Hannah)*   'Cause he's a loser.

HANNAH *(Overlapping, to twin #1)*   Ohh!

MICKEY *(Overlapping, gesturing)*   H-he's so awkward and he's clumsy like me . . .

HANNAH *(Overlapping, chuckling)*   I know, I know.

MICKEY *(Overlapping)* . . . so I, so I like that. I always like an underconfident person . . .

HANNAH *(Overlapping, touching the mitt and reacting)*   That's really nice!

MICKEY *(Still rambling on, gesturing to Hannah)*   . . . you know? I, uh . . .

HANNAH *(Overlapping)*   You know, he's been wanting a mitt. *She helps twin #2 open his present. It's a football.*

MICKEY   You've always had good taste in husbands, so . . .

HANNAH *(Chuckling and nodding)*   Thanks, thanks.

MICKEY Mm-hm.

HANNAH *(Leaning down to look at the football)* That's a beauty!

MICKEY Isn't that great?

HANNAH Oh!

MICKEY *(Pointing, to twin #2)* Go right over there.

HANNAH Football!
Twin #2, panting, runs offscreen to catch the football.

MICKEY *(To the offscreen twin)* Come on! Hurry up! Let's go!

HANNAH *(Looking offscreen at twin #2)* Wow!

MICKEY *(Still pointing, gearing up for the pass)* Go out, go out by the Sung vase and, and catch this.
Mickey throws the football.

MICKEY See? *(Whistling)*

HANNAH *(Pointing offscreen)* Hey, d— Watch, watch the picture.
There's a sound of breaking glass. Hannah and Mickey react.

CUT TO:
EXTERIOR. NEW YORK CITY STREET—DAY.

Mickey is walking up a West Side street, his hands in his coat pockets. Jazz plays in the background as he talks over the screen.

MICKEY'S VOICE-OVER Gee, Hannah's sweet. Although, sometimes I still do get angry when I think of things. Oh, what the hell. At least, I'm not paying child support. *(Sighing)* Oh, God, I hope there's nothing physically wrong with me, either.
Mickey pushes open the outside door of Dr. Abel's office, as the movie cuts to the doctor's consultation room. The doctor is framed in the doorway, looking through a file cabinet.

DR. ABEL *(Taking out Mickey's file)* So what's the, uh, problem this time?

MICKEY *(Offscreen)* This time I really think I have something.
While Mickey answers him offscreen, Dr. Abel turns and walks towards him. The camera follows the doctor's movements from the other side of the wall, obscuring him briefly. It moves across a dark examining-room wall to a second doorway, where Mickey sits on a stool, continuing to talk to the offscreen Dr. Abel.

MICKEY *(Onscreen)* I mean, I'm absolutely convinced that-that— You know, I mean, it's not like that adenoidal thing, you know, where I didn't realize I had them out.
Dr. Abel walks back onscreen. Both he and Mickey are now seen through the second doorway. Dr. Abel sniffs and stands directly in front of the sitting Mickey. He stares down at him as Mickey talks.

MICKEY *(Continuing, gesturing)* So, so, but it was when I was younger, so—

DR. ABEL *(Overlapping, interrupting)* You know, I saw your father this week about his sinus . . .

MICKEY *(Folding his arms on his chest)* Mm-hm.

DR. ABEL *(Continuing)* . . . and, uh, he complained of chest pains.

MICKEY Well, this guy's the real hypochondriac of the family. I mean, he's, you know, he's—

DR. ABEL *(Interrupting)* You mentioned on the phone that you'd had some dizziness.

MICKEY *(Rubbing his hands on his knees)* Yes, a little dizziness, and I think, I think I'm developing a hearing loss in my right ear *(Poking at his ears and gesturing)* . . . or my left ear, my, my left

. . . oh, n-n-n-no. No, I'm sorry. It was my right, my right, my right or my left ear.
Dr. Abel chuckles.

MICKEY *(Nodding and gesturing)*   Now I ca-can't remember.

DR. ABEL   Let's take a look.
An uptempo big-band sound is heard as the movie cuts to Mickey's examination, beginning with a close-up of Dr. Abel using an otoscope to examine the ear of a nervous Mickey. Next is a hearing test. The film shows the doctors's hands turning the dials on a sonometer. Mickey sits on a nearby high stool, large earphones on his head. He listens with such concentration that he squints his eyes. He holds up a finger in response to the sounds he hears in his headset. Finally, the film shows Dr. Abel hitting a large tuning fork with his finger. He puts the vibrating fork to Mickey's ear. Mickey, looking up at the offscreen doctor's face, nods.

The music stops as the film cuts back to Dr. Abel's consultation room. Dr. Abel walks from the examining room, through the consultation room, to a second examining room across the way. He talks to the offscreen Mickey as he walks.

DR. ABEL   Well, I'm sorry to say you have had a significant drop in the high-decibel range of your right ear.

MICKEY *(Offscreen)*   Really?!
Dr. Abel moves offscreen in the second examining room. The camera stays focused on the doorway to this room as the doctor and Mickey talk offscreen.

DR. ABEL *(Offscreen)*   Have you been exposed to a loud noise recently, or did you have a virus?

MICKEY *(Offscreen)*   No, I-I've been perfectly healthy. You know me.
Dr. Abel briefly passes by the doorway.

MICKEY *(Offscreen)*   I always, I-I always imagine that I have things.

DR. ABEL *(Offscreen)*   When did you first notice this?

MICKEY *(Offscreen)*   Oh, uh, about a month ago. Wha-what do I have?
Looking preoccupied, Dr. Abel walks back into the consultation room, holding Mickey's open file. He strides over to his desk, revealing a frightened Mickey, sitting in a chair opposite it. Still standing, the doctor leans over the desk, his back to the camera, and makes a few notes in the file.

DR. ABEL   You've had some dizzy spells. *(Sighing)* What about ringing and buzzing? Have you, uh, noticed any of that?

MICKEY *(Gesturing)*   Yes, now-now that you mention it, uh, I-I-I have, uh, buzzing and also ringing. Ringing and buzzing. Um, am I going deaf, or something?

DR. ABEL *(Making more notes in the file)*   And it's just in one ear?

MICKEY *(Picking at his fingers)*   Yes, is it, is it, uh, healthier to have problems in both ears?
Dr. Abel chuckles as he closes Mickey's file and straightens up. The camera looks past his back and shoulders to the anxious Mickey.

DR. ABEL *(His face offscreen)*   What I'd like to do, is to make an appointment for you at the hospital. I'd like to have them run some tests.

MICKEY   The hospital? What kind of tests?
Dr. Abel lays his pen across Mickey's closed file. He walks around his desk and sits on its edge close to Mickey.

DR. ABEL *(Sighing)*   Now, don't get alarmed. These are just more sophisticated audiometry tests than I can run here. *(Gesturing)* I mean, it's, it's nothing.

MICKEY *(Gesturing)*   Well, if it's nothing, then why do I have to go into the hosptial at all? I mean, uh, I hear perfectly fine, so I'm, so I'm a little weak on the, on the high decibels. So I, you know, I won't go to the opera.

DR. ABEL *(Sniffing)*   You know, there's no reason for panic. I just want to rule out some things.

MICKEY   Like what?

DR. ABEL *(Shaking his head)*   It's nothing. Will you trust me?

CUT TO:
EXTERIOR. STREET CORNER—DAY.

Mickey stands in a telephone booth on a corner near Dr. Abel's office; he talks on the phone. It is raining. A man and a woman holding an umbrella pass by; traffic moves across a nearby intersection.

MICKEY *(Into the telephone)*   Huh, uh, hello, Dr. Wilkes? Dr. Wilkes, this is Mickey Sachs. You have a minute? I want to ask you a question.
The film cuts to Dr. Wilkes, on the telephone at his end. He is in his office; he leans back in his chair, dangling his stethescope as he speaks. Behind him, a chest X-ray is mounted on a light panel.

DR. WILKES *(Into the telephone)*   Sure, Mickey. What's up?
The movie cuts back and forth between Mickey in his phone booth asking questions and Dr. Wilkes in his office answering them.

MICKEY *(Into the telephone, gesturing)*   I-if you have, i-if you have a hearing loss in one ear, and-and it's not from a, uh, virus or a loud noise or anything, wh-what are the possibilities?

DR. WILKES *(Into his telephone)*   Anything. Uh, often it's heredi-tary. Flu, uh, even a small noise will do it.

MICKEY *(Into the telephone)*   Uh, right, but-but nothing worse?

DR. WILKES *(Into the telephone)*   Well, yes, I guess the, uh, dark side of the spectrum is a brain tumor.

MICKEY *(Into the telephone, reacting with a blank stare)*   Really?

CUT TO:
INTERIOR. MICKEY'S OFFICE — NIGHT.

Gail, wearing her glasses, stands behind a crowded but well-ordered desk. Two assistants, a man and a woman, stand around her.

GAIL *(Handing them each some pages of script)*   Okay, so here's the new pages.

WOMAN *(Looking over the pages)*   Say, did cards get these?

GAIL *(Scratching her head)*   No, not yet. No.

MAN *(Looking over his pages)*   Well, let's hope it's good.

GAIL   Yeah, really. Really.
The assistants walk off. As they leave, Gail calls out after them.

GAIL   Eh, we'll be down in a minute, okay?
The telephone starts to ring, Gail pauses, looking offscreen. She takes off her glasses and squints.

GAIL   Mickey, what's the matter with you? You're all white!
The film cuts to Mickey, who is pacing and wringing his hands. He walks over to Gail. The phone continues to ring.

MICKEY   I feel dizzy. Sshh, you know, I don't feel well.
He starts to pant, looking worriedly around the room. He continues to wring his hands as Gail stares at him, concerned.

MICKEY   Do you hear a ringing? Is there, is there a, is there a ringing sound? *(Sighing)*

GAIL *(Gesturing)*   Yeah. Yeah, yeah. I hear, I hear it.
She sits down and picks up the phone.

MICKEY *(Shaking his head)* N-n-no, not that.

GAIL *(Overlapping, into the telephone)* Hello?

MICKEY *(Covering first one ear, then the other, continuing)* Like—
(Putting a finger into his ear, closing his eyes and listening)

GAIL *(Into the telephone)* Uh, yeah, yeah. We're going to be working late tonight. N-no, we'll order out. It's all right. Yeah.
Gail hangs up the phone.

MICKEY *(Turning to Gail, gesturing nervously)* Sssss, if I have a brain tumor, I don't know what I'm gonna do. *(Sighing)*

GAIL You don't have a brain tumor. He didn't say you had a brain tumor.

MICKEY *(Sighing)* No, naturally *(Gesturing)* they're not gonna tell you, because, well, you know, th—, sometimes the weaker ones will panic if you tell 'em.

GAIL *(Pointing a finger at Mickey)* But not you.

MICKEY *(Flinging up his arms, sighing)* Oh, God! *(Looking around worriedly and touching Gail's shoulder)* Do you hear a buzzing? Is there a buzzing?
He pants and begins to pace around the room. The camera follows him as he walks away from Gail.

GAIL *(Impatiently)* Mickey, come on, we got a show to do!

MICKEY *(Pacing)* I can't keep my mind on the show.

GAIL *(Offscreen)* But there's nothing wrong with you.

MICKEY *(Sighing and gesturing)* If there's nothing wrong with me *(Pacing back to the desk and Gail)* then why does he want me to come back for tests?!

GAIL *(Gesturing)* Well, he has to rule out certain things. *(Sighing)*

MICKEY Like what?! What?

GAIL *(Shrugging)* I don't know. Cancer, I—

MICKEY *(Interrupting)* Don't say that! I don't want to hear that word! *(Gesturing)* Don't mention that while I'm in the building.

GAIL *(Gesturing)* But you don't have any symptoms!

MICKEY *(Gesturing)* You— I got the classic symptoms of a brain tumor!
Mickey sighs.

GAIL Two months ago, you thought you had a malignant melanoma.

MICKEY *(Gesturing)* Naturally, I, I— Do you know I— The sudden appearance of a black spot on my back!

GAIL It was on your shirt!

MICKEY *(Sighing)* I— How was I to know?! *(Pointing to his back)* Everyone was pointing back here.
He sighs again as Gail, frustrated, gestures impatiently to the papers on the desk.

GAIL Come on, we've got to make some booking decisions.
Mickey begins pacing around the room again. He wrings his hands and blows on them.

MICKEY I can't. I can't think of it. This morning, I was so happy, you know. Now I, I don't know what went wrong. *(Sighing)*

GAIL Eh, you were miserable this morning! We got bad reviews, terrible ratings, the sponsors are furious . . .

MICKEY *(Pacing back to the desk, still wringing his hands)* No, I was happy, but I just didn't realize I was happy.

CUT TO:

The Stanislavski Catering Company in action.

Sophisticated pop music plays as the film cuts to:

INTERIOR. LOFT—DAY.

An abstract painting on a wall fills the screen. Light laughter is heard, as well as the sophisticated music; offscreen brunch guests chatter indistinctly.

FEMALE BRUNCH GUEST *(Offscreen)* These things are delicious! What in the world are they?
Holly walks onto the screen in front of the painting. She holds an almost empty tray of hors d'oeuvres; she wears a uniform.

HOLLY   Oh, um, those are quail eggs.

FEMALE BRUNCH GUEST *(Offscreen)*   Oh, they're very good.
Holly walks past the painting towards the female brunch guest. A man walks in front of her. Chatter, light laughter, and music are still heard; a party is in progress.

HOLLY *(Nodding)*   Yeah, my friend April makes those. *(Holding out the tray)*   Here, try the shrimp puffs. These are delicious.

FEMALE BRUNCH GUEST *(Taking one from the tray)*   Oh, thank you. That looks great.

HOLLY   I make those.

FEMALE BRUNCH GUEST   Mmm. Thanks.
Holly laughs lightly as she walks away from the woman. Holding her tray, she passes a large oval loft window and several clusters of brunch guests. They are eating and drinking. No one pays any attention to her.

HOLLY *(To two male guests in her way)*   Excuse me.
One of the men, murmuring his thanks, takes a last shrimp puff as Holly passes.

HOLLY *(To the man)*   Thank you.
Holly finally makes her way into the cluttered loft kitchen. Her tray is empty.

APRIL *(Offscreen)*   The Stroganoff is ready.
Holly, excited, runs over to April, who is busy taking the Stroganoff out of the oven. She wears the same uniform as Holly: black skirt, white shirt, and black bowtie.

HOLLY *(Animatedly)*   We're a big hit.

APRIL   Oh, in this we're a big hit. Yesterday I auditioned for *Come Back Little Sheba*. That, I wasn't such a big hit.
April, holding the Stroganoff, dashes out of the kitchen to serve the

party guests. Holly calls after her, offscreen, as David walks past the hurrying April into the kitchen.

HOLLY *(Offscreen)* You will be. You will be. You'll get five jobs next week.
David walks over to Holly, who is busy at the pot- and pan-covered stove.

DAVID *(To Holly)* Excuse me, are there any more clams?

HOLLY *(Gesturing at some canapés warming on the stove)* Only a few. A few. *(Chuckling as David takes one)* Do you like 'em?

DAVID I can't resist.

HOLLY *(Busily working at the stove)* Really? How flattering! Did you try the shrimp puffs?

DAVID *(Eating a canapé and pointing at Holly)* Listen, you guys are too attractive to be caterers. Something's wrong.

HOLLY We're actresses.

DAVID   Is this your first job?

HOLLY *(Grabbing a quiche from an overhead stove)*   Really? Is the food that bad?

DAVID *(Shaking his head)*   Oh no. Not at all.
As Holly carries the quiche outside to the party, April comes back into the kitchen from another doorway. Music, as well as the chatter of mingling guests, is heard in the background.

APRIL   We need more bread and some baked lasa— *(Realizing Holly isn't there and, at the same time, noticing David)* uh, lasagne. *(Turning to David)* Hi.

DAVID *(Standing by the sink as he wipes his hands and mouth with a napkin)*   I know. You're an actress with a great flair for shrimp puffs.

APRIL *(Working at the stove, pointing a finger for emphasis)*   Uh, no, the shrimp puffs are Holly's. I do the, uh, crêpes caviar.
She walks past David to a counter where she begins to fold napkins. David leans back against the sink.

DAVID   And the quail is responsible for the quail eggs.

APRIL *(Turning to David and chuckling)*   Well, let's hope so.
Holly enters the kitchen holding out a plate of clams. She walks over to David.

HOLLY   Here, I stole you a couple of extra clams.

DAVID *(Taking the plate)*   Ah!

HOLLY *(Looking busily around the room)*   Now.

DAVID *(Overlapping, gesturing)*   Incidentally, I'm David Tolchin.

APRIL *(Turning to David)*   Oh, uh, April Knox. Hi.
They shake hands.

DAVID *(Looking at her)*   Hi.

APRIL *(Leaving the counter and squeezing past David and Holly)*   Oh.

HOLLY *(Overlapping, moving out of April's way)*   I'm sorry.
April walks offscreen to another area of the kitchen. Holly picks up a napkin from the crowded table.

DAVID *(Overlapping Holly's apology, turning to her)*   You're Holly.

HOLLY *(Nodding, looking at David as she wipes her hands with the napkin)*   Yeah, we're the Stanislavski Catering Company.

DAVID *(Chewing on a clam canapé)*   Now I'm going to tell you the truth. I really came in here because I was bored stiff by the party.

HOLLY *(Laughing, still wiping her hands)*   What makes you think we're more interesting?
David walks around the table, putting the plate of clams down on the already crowded surface. Holly follows him, chuckling, throwing her napkin into an offscreen garbage can as David stops at a small television set near the doorway. Guests in the other room can be seen chatting together in clusters.

DAVID *(Turning on the set)*   Actually, I'm going to listen to *Aida*, if I'm not getting in your way.
Canned laughter and miscellaneous chatter is heard from the television set. David watches the set, still munching on a clam, while Holly and April reassure him offscreen.

APRIL *(Offscreen)*   No . . . no. N— *(Sniffing)*

HOLLY *(Offscreen, overlapping)*   Not at all.
David checks his wristwatch as Holly walks over to him.

HOLLY *(Gesturing, fiddling with another napkin)*   We saw, um, Pavarotti, eh, uh, in *Ernani* at the Met, and I cried . . .

DAVID *(Nodding, his hand still on his watch as he looks at Holly)* I cry at the opera.

APRIL *(Offscreen)* Oh, I-I-I go limp in the last scene in *La Traviata*. Limp.
Holly chuckles as David, listening to April, impressed, walks over to her. She is standing by the table.

DAVID *(Nodding, to April)* Me, too. I have a private box at the Met. *(Gesturing)* I bring my little bottle of wine, I open it, I sit there and I watch and *(Glancing over to the offscreen Holly)* I cry. It's disgusting.
April chuckles as Holly walks back onscreen; she is busy preparing another tray of hors d'oeuvres.

HOLLY *(Gesturing)* Oh, what, what do you do?

DAVID *(Nodding)* I'm an architect.

APRIL Wha— *(Turning to glance at Holly)* What kind of things do you build?

DAVID   Are you really interested?

APRIL   Yeah.

HOLLY *(Nodding)* Yeah.

DAVID   What time do you get off?
The three exchange glances. Holly shrugs.

CUT TO:
EXTERIOR. A MANHATTAN STREET—DAY.

A contemporary red building, designed by David, is seen, squeezed in between two older buildings. Holly, April, and David talk offscreen.

HOLLY *(Offscreen)*   Wow, it's the red one?

APRIL *(Offscreen)*   Oh, it's magnificent!

DAVID *(Offscreen)*   Yeah.

HOLLY *(Offscreen)*   It's terrific!
The film moves down from the buildings to reveal the trio sitting in David's Jaguar across the street. David and April sit in the front seat; Holly sits scrunched up in back, her head slightly forward.

DAVID *(Gesturing, looking back and forth from the buildings to Holly and April)*   The design's deliberately noncontextural. But I wanted to . . . keep the atmosphere of the street, you know, and the proportions.

HOLLY *(Nodding)*   Uh-huh.

DAVID   And in the material. That's . . . that's unpolished red granite. *(Pausing as he watches Holly and April's reaction)*

HOLLY   Oh!

APRIL *(Overlapping)*   Oh, is that what it is?

HOLLY *(Starting to speak)*   Uh—

APRIL *(Interrupting, nodding at Holly)* I-i-it has an o-organic quality, you know.

HOLLY *(Nodding, overlapping)* Right.

APRIL *(Looking back at the building with reverence)* It's almost . . . almost, uhhh, entirely wholly interdependent, if you know what I mean. I-I . . . I can't put it into words. The important thing is-is-is it-it breathes.

DAVID *(Turning to April, emphatically)* You know, April, people pass by vital structures in this city all the time, and they never take the time to appreciate them. I get the feeling you tune in to your environment.

APRIL *(Shaking her head)* Oh—

HOLLY *(Interrupting, gesturing and nodding)* Oh, it's really important.
David turns and briefly glances at Holly; he then turns back to April.

APRIL *(Looking only at David)* What are your favorite buildings, David?

DAVID You want to see some?

APRIL *(Nodding)* Oh, yeah.

DAVID Well, let's do it.

APRIL *(Looking at David)* Great.
David starts the car and the movie cuts to an unfolding visual excursion through New York City's landmark buildings, as seen from the trio's point of view in the moving Jaguar. Inspiring classical music plays in the background.

The series of shots includes the Dakota, complete with surrounding winter trees, the Graybar building on Lexington Avenue, an incredibly ornate building on Seventh Avenue and Fifty-eighth Street, a red-stone church, an old building with embellished, bulging windows on West Forty-fourth Street, the Art Deco Chrysler Building, a red-brick building, Abigail Adams's old stone house, and the Pomander Walk nestled off Broadway on the Upper West Side. The group can be seen walking down the path between the old-fashioned row houses and shrubbery. A lamppost sits in the foreground.

It is now dark. The music continues to play as the film cuts to the façade of a rococo-style building, complete with French doors and ornate windows. The admiring group is heard offscreen.

HOLLY *(Offscreen)*   Oh, it's just so romantic. I just want to put on a long gown . . .

DAVID *(Offscreen, overlapping)*   Yes.

HOLLY *(Offscreen, continuing)*   . . . and open the French doors and go on the balcony—

APRIL *(Offscreen, interrupting)*   It's French, though. It really is.

HOLLY *(Offscreen)*   Yeah.

APRIL *(Offscreen, overlapping)*   It feels like you're in France.

DAVID *(Offscreen, overlapping)*   It-it is. It's romantic.
   The music stops. The screen, which has been exploring the rococo building's façade, now shows the equally elegant building alongside it.

DAVID *(Offscreen)*   And it's got a handsome partner sitting right beside it.

HOLLY *(Offscreen)*   Yeah.

DAVID *(Offscreen, overlapping)*   They fit right in together. And your eye goes along, lulled into complacency, and then . . .
   The film moves from the two elegant façades to show an ugly, ultra-modern structure covered with tiny, diamond-shaped motifs.

APRIL *(Offscreen)*   That's just—

DAVID *(Offscreen, interrupting)*   Look at this.

HOLLY *(Offscreen)*   That's disgusting!

APRIL *(Offscreen, continuing)*   . . . a monstrosity! Who would do that?

HOLLY *(Offscreen, overlapping)*   It's really terrible.

DAVID *(Offscreen, emphatically)*   It's really sad.

HOLLY *(Offscreen)*   And it ruins everything else.

DAVID *(Offscreen, agreeing)*   It does.
The film moves from the ugly façade to the building's equally ugly entrance. A large car is parked right in front of the building.

APRIL *(Offscreen)*   Well . . . we have seen a lot of stuff today, though.

HOLLY *(Offscreen, chuckling)*   Yeah.

DAVID *(Offscreen, overlapping)*   Yeah.

APRIL *(Offscreen, overlapping)*   A lot of works.
The group is now seen walking down the canopied entrance stairs of an apartment house on the other side of the street, where they'd been gazing at both the lovely and ugly façades across the way. David is in the lead; the women follow, Holly slightly behind April.

HOLLY *(Nodding)*   Yeah.

DAVID *(Glancing at his watch)*   Maybe we should start thinking about going home, huh?

HOLLY   Fast.

APRIL   Oh, geez, yeah.

HOLLY *(Overlapping)*   Okay.
They walk towards the car.

DAVID *(Looking back at the women as he walks around the car to the driver's side)* Uh, who gets dropped first?

APRIL Uh—

HOLLY *(Overlapping, looking at April)* Oh, gee, I don't know. Um . . .

DAVID *(Offscreen, overlapping)* Well . . .

APRIL *(Overlapping)* Well, I live downtown.

HOLLY *(Glancing at April)* Yeah, I, we both live downtown.
David leans over the roof of the car, looking at the women, waiting for their decision.

APRIL *(Gesturing)* Uh . . .

HOLLY *(To David)* It depends on what way you want to go.

APRIL *(Overlapping)* Well, wait. You know what? I know.

HOLLY Uh . . .

APRIL *(To Holly, gesturing)* If . . . well, if we took the, if we took Fifth, then-then-then we'd get to your house first, yeah?

DAVID *(Overlapping, nodding)* We could . . . we could do that.

HOLLY *(Nodding)* Right. Yeah, but Fifth is so jammed, isn't it?
She looks at David.

APRIL *(Overlapping, to Holly)* Well, sometimes, some, uh . . .

HOLLY *(Interrupting)* I mean, it's jammed. If we went . . . um . . .
Both she and April mumble awkwardly.

DAVID *(Pointing to Holly, interrupting their chatter)* Y-you live in Chelsea, don't you?

HOLLY *(Nodding at David)* Yes.

DAVID Well, I-I guess if you live in Chelsea, that's probably first.

HOLLY *(Nodding nervously)* Oh, okay.

APRIL Yeah.

DAVID And then, uh, April . . . huh?

APRIL *(Overlapping, nodding)* Great.
They get into the car. Once again Holly's in the backseat. The classical music begins anew.

The movie cuts briefly to cut to the traffic and lights of a Manhattan avenue as seen from the moving Jaguar. It then moves to a close-up of Holly, sitting in the backseat, her head near the window. She is staring straight ahead.

HOLLY'S VOICE-OVER Naturally I get taken home first. Well, obviously he prefers April. Of course I was so tongue-tied all night. I can't believe I said that about the Guggenheim. My stupid little roller-skating joke. I should never tell jokes. Mom can tell 'em and Hannah, but I kill 'em. *(Glaring at the offscreen April's back)* Where did April come up with that stuff about Adolph Loos and terms like "organic form"? *(Looking out the side window, pausing for a moment)* Well, naturally. She went to Brandeis.
The movie cuts to Holly's point of view: the front seat where David and April sit, the Jaguar's windshield, and the passing lights and traffic of the street. Holly continues her ruminations as April leans over to say something to David.

HOLLY'S VOICE-OVER But I don't think she knows what she's talking about. Could you believe the way she was calling him David? "Yes, David. I feel that way, too, David. What a marvelous space, David." *(Emphatically)* I hate April. She's pushy.
The film moves back to Holly in the backseat, still lost in thought.

HOLLY'S VOICE-OVER Now they'll dump me and she'll invite him up. I blew it. *(Sighing, looking out the side window)* And I really like him a lot. Oh, screw it. I'm not gonna get all upset. I've got reading to do tonight. You know, maybe I'll get into bed early. I'll turn on a movie and take an extra Seconal.

The classical music stops and some uptempo jazz begins. The screen cuts to black and a title appears.

"... nobody, not even the rain, has such small hands."

CUT TO:
EXTERIOR. STREET OUTSIDE FREDERICK'S LOFT—DAY.

The movie briefly holds on a ripped, red, paint-splattered door as Elliot, wearing a raincoat, appears nearby. He looks down the street and the film cuts to his point of view: Frederick's loft building.

The movie goes back to the impatient Elliot; he's looking around him. He glances at his watch as the film cuts back once again to the loft building, where Lee finally appears, walking down the street away from Elliot. A truck passes down the street. Lee doesn't see him. She walks further and further away; she turns a corner.

Elliot frantically looks around again; then, in a burst of decision, he runs around a garbage dump, crossing the street, and still running, he moves down an adjacent street, past The Canal Lumber Company and several other buildings, as the film cuts back to Lee, walking down a different street, oblivious.

The jazz plays on as the movie cuts back and forth between the fast-moving Elliot, rushing down the SoHo streets, past a truck waiting for a light to change, past some pedestrians, some garbage cans, turning corners, and the strolling Lee, walking up different streets, past different buildings.

Lee eventually crosses a street, lost in thought, looking right and left, as Elliot, pretending nonchalance, waits on the corner, looking at his watch. She looks up in surprise; the music stops.

ELLIOT *(Trying not to sound out of breath)* Oh, my goodness!

LEE *(Overlapping, smiling in surprise)* Oh, Elliot!

ELLIOT Hi.

LEE *(Smiling)* What are you doing here?

ELLIOT *(Looking around, gesturing)* Well, I'm-I'm looking for a bookstore.

LEE *(Shaking her head)* Oh, what, in this section of town?

ELLIOT Yes. Yeah, I-I'm kill—

LEE *(Overlapping)* You're out looking here?

ELLIOT *(Glancing at his watch again)*   Well, yes, I'm killing time. I have a client near here and I . . . I'm quite early.

LEE *(Laughing)*   Ohhhh!

ELLIOT *(Gesturing)*   How about you?

LEE   Oh. Well, I live—

ELLIOT *(Interrupting, chuckling)*   Oh, yes! You live near here, don't you?

LEE *(Overlapping, chuckling)*   Yes, I do.

ELLIOT *(Putting his hands behind his back)*   Where are you headed?

LEE   Oh, I was just going to my AA meeting.

ELLIOT   Oh, my goodness. Well, why do you still go to those? You never touch alcohol.
They begin to walk down the street.

LEE *(Laughing)*   Well, listen, you didn't know me before Frederick. I'd . . . I'd start with a beer at about ten in the morning,
and . . . go on.

ELLIOT *(Looking at Lee)*   Oh. You must have been, uh, very unhappy.

LEE   Yeah, unhappy and fat. *(Chuckling)* And I still find the
meetings very comforting, you know.
She shrugs.

ELLIOT   I'll never understand it. You're so bright and charming
and beautiful.

LEE *(Laughing)*   Oh, God.

ELLIOT *(Overlapping, chuckling)*   I think to myself *(Laughing)* what
problems could she possibly have?

LEE *(Gesturing, laughing)*   Don't let me get started on my child-
hood. *(Stopping in her tracks, remembering)* Oh, you know what?
There *is* a bookstore.

ELLIOT *(Stopping alongside her)*   Yes?

LEE *(Overlapping, pointing)*   A couple of blocks from here. If you
don't know about it, you should. You'd really love it.

ELLIOT   Yes?

LEE *(Nodding)*   Yeah, you would.

ELLIOT *(Looking around for a moment, then gesturing to Lee)*   Well,
i-if-if you have some free time . . .

LEE *(Nodding)*   Yeah, sure. *(Chuckling)*

ELLIOT   Thank you.
*They begin to walk again as the movie cuts to the interior of the
Pageant Book & Print Shop, an old, serious bookstore. A nude print*

hangs at the end of one of the library shelf-like bookcases, which are packed, row after row, with books. An unseen Elliot and Lee carry on a conversation as the camera moves down an aisle, past the rows of books. A piano playing "Bewitched" is heard. Pictures hang on the aisle ends of the shelves.

LEE *(Offscreen)* Isn't this great? *(Chuckling)* They have everything here.

ELLIOT *(Offscreen, distracted)* Yes, it's-it's wonderful.

LEE *(Offscreen)* What book did you want to buy?

ELLIOT *(Offscreen)* What? Book?

LEE *(Offscreen)* Your book? You wanted to buy a book?
The camera moves past another aisle of books to reveal Lee, browsing through a shelf.

ELLIOT *(Offscreen)* Oh, book? Oh, no, I . . . *(Laughing)* I'm killing time. I . . . I-I just, uh, w-want to browse, uh . . .

LEE *(Looking up at a row of books)* Well, you sure picked the right place. I mean, you can stay here all afternoon, not buy anything and just read.
She walks down a center aisle, the camera still in its parallel aisle, following her.

ELLIOT *(Offscreen)* Unless, of course, if-if you had some time, I mean, we could get some coffee.

LEE No, I don't have time.
Lee stops at the row where Elliot has been browsing. She is hidden by a shelf; only Elliot is seen as he talks to the offscreen Lee.

ELLIOT *(Gesturing)* No, no. I-I-I understand completely. No problem. Y-you're busy. I-I-I . . .

LEE *(Offscreen, chuckling)*   You seem tense. Is everything all right? You feel okay?

ELLIOT *(Overlapping)*   No! No . . .

LEE *(Offscreen)*   No?

ELLIOT *(Gesturing, looking at books)*   Uh, yes!

LEE *(Offscreen)*   Yes?
Elliot starts walking down the center aisle, in the same direction Lee had walked up. He continues to talk to her as she remains offscreen in a nearby row.

ELLIOT *(Offscreen momentarily, hidden by a shelf as he talks)*   Yes.

LEE *(Offscreen)*   Everything's okay? *(Chuckling)*

ELLIOT   Yeah. How are you?

LEE *(Offscreen)*   I'm . . . all right.

ELLIOT *(Offscreen momentarily, hidden by another shelf as he walks)*   How-how's Frederick?
Elliot stops walking to browse through some books. "Bewitched" still plays.

LEE *(Offscreen)*   Fine. Oh, we went to the Caravaggio exhibition at the Met. It's such a treat to go through a museum with Frederick. I mean . . . you learn so much. Do you like Caravaggio?

ELLIOT *(Turning to talk to the offscreen Lee)*   Oh, yes. Who doesn't? *(Pointing)* Look!
Elliot turns and walks back down the center aisle to a row of books he'd already passed.

ELLIOT *(Pointing to a book on a shelf, continuing)*   e. e. cummings. I'd like to get you this.

LEE *(Offscreen, laughing)* Oh, no, I can't let you get me that. That's too much.

ELLIOT *(Pulling the book off the shelf and browsing through it)* Oh, oh, yes. I-I-I'd like to, uh, uh, very much.

LEE *(Offscreen)* No, I don't think so.

ELLIOT *(Gesturing with the book, looking at the offscreen Lee)* I-I read a poem of you and thought of his last week. *(Nervously laughing, trying to correct his mistake)* A poem of *(Laughing)* his and thought of *you* last— *(Laughing)* You'll be fine, though. *(Chuckling)*
Lee walks over to Elliot in the center aisle. She looks at the book.

LEE *(Overlapping)* Uh, uh, this is great. I mean, I love e. e. cummings, but I can't let you get this.

ELLIOT *(Overlapping, patting the book)* Yes, I'd . . . I-I-I'd love, I'd love to get you this.

LEE *(Looking down at the book)* Well, sure.

ELLIOT *(Overlapping)* And-and maybe, um . . . maybe we could discuss it sometime.
He hands Lee the book. She thumbs through it, as the movie cuts to:

The street outside the bookstore. Lee, holding the book in a brown bag, and Elliot are walking out.

LEE *(Laughing, holding up the bag)* Well, thanks a lot.

ELLIOT *(Pointing to the bookstore)* Thanks for showing me the bookstore. Perhaps you could, uh, take me to an AA meeting sometime. Uh . . . uh, I'd love to see what goes on.

LEE *(Nodding)* Well, yeah, yeah. You'd love it. It's really entertaining. You'd have a good time. *(Stepping closer to the curb and hailing a cab)* I know you would.

ELLIOT *(Pointing to the book)*   And, uh, d-don't forget the poem on page a hundred and twelve. It reminded me of you.
A taxi pulls over to the curb; they walk over to it.

LEE *(Laughing)*   Really? Well . . .
Elliot opens the rear door for Lee. She laughs as she gets in.

ELLIOT *(Leaning down to talk to Lee in the cab)*   Page a hundred and twelve.

LEE   Bye.

ELLIOT *(Closing the taxi door for Lee)*   Bye.
He watches the taxi pull away.

CUT TO:
INTERIOR. FREDERICK'S LOFT BEDROOM—NIGHT.

Lee, in slacks and shirt, is curled up on the bed, her back to the camera, as she reads the e. e. cummings poem in the glow of a night-table lamp. The piano music is still heard.

LEE'S VOICE-OVER *(Reading)*   "your slightest look easily will / unclose me / though I have closed myself as / fingers, / you open always petal by petal / myself . . ."
As Lee continues to read aloud, the movie cuts to Elliot's darkened den, lit by a light in the hallway. Elliot enters, wearing a robe, crossing the room in the dark.

LEE'S VOICE-OVER *(Continuing reading)*   ". . . as Spring opens / (touching skillfully, mysteriously) / her first rose / (i do not know what it is about you / that closes and opens; / only something in me understands / the voice of your eyes is deeper than / all roses) . . ."
Elliot turns on a light. The camera stays on his face as he looks off into the distance, mouthing indistinctly the line of poetry Lee next reads aloud.

LEE'S VOICE-OVER *(Continuing reading)* "nobody, not even the rain, has such small hands."
The film leaves Elliot's face and cuts back to the loft, where Lee, having finished the poem, sits up in the bed, staring pensively, lost in her thoughts.

CUT TO:

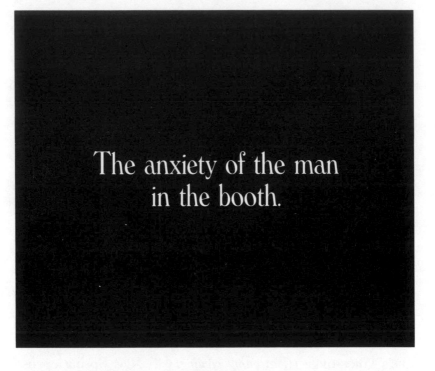

The anxiety of the man
in the booth.

Upbeat jazz begins to play and the film cuts to:

The façade of Mount Sinai Hospital. It is day. A few cars whiz by as the film moves inside, to various scenes depicting Mickey's comprehensive exam.

First is a hearing test, and the movie cuts to a darkened hearing-test room. A light goes on, revealing a slouched-over Mickey sitting in a glass booth. He is wearing a set of headphones. The camera moves back, revealing a technician at the console on the other side of the booth. Mickey signals with his finger when he hears a sound on his headset. The jazz continues.

Next is an electronystagmography (ENG). Graph paper rolls out of a machine, and after a brief glimpse of the rolling paper, the camera moves over to show Mickey lying terrified, without his glasses, on a couch, with electrodes stuck all over his head.

The film then cuts to a BSER test room, where Mickey, sitting in a corner chair, wears another set of headphones. An electrode is attached to his forehead; a nearby technician sits at a computer video screen, looking at a monitoring graph.

Last but not least is the tomography. Over the shoulders of a technician in a booth, a large window displays a huge, white rotating machine. It makes a whooshing noise as it turns. The camera moves down the giant cranelike device to reveal Mickey, once again lying down, this time on a table, his eyes closed, underneath it.

CUT TO:
INTERIOR. DR. GREY'S OFFICE—DAY.

A sitting Dr. Grey, his back to the camera, is examining a group of X-rays clipped to the light board behind his desk.

DR. GREY   I wasn't too happy with the results of your ENG or your BSER either.
The doctor turns his chair around to face a tense Mickey sitting on the other side of his desk.

DR. GREY   Uh, which is why I sent you to Tomography, which was all that stuff you saw rolling around. *(Pointing to a spot on one of the X-rays)* You see this little gray area here?
Mickey stares at the X-ray, horrified.

DR. GREY   That gray area's what I had hoped that we wouldn't run into. I'd like you to come in Monday morning for, uh, a CAT scan.

MICKEY *(Reacting)*   A brain scan?

DR. GREY *(Gesturing)*   Mr. Sachs, let's take one step at a time. We won't make any decisions until we have all the information in front of us, all right?

CUT TO:
EXTERIOR. MOUNT SINAI HOSPITAL—DAY.

Mickey is seen leaving the hospital. He strides slowly, his shoulders slouched, his hands in his pockets. His voice is heard over the screen as he crosses the street, continuing his self-absorbed walk on the opposite side. Occasional traffic goes by.

MICKEY'S VOICE-OVER   Okay . . . take it easy. He didn't say you had anything. He just doesn't like the spot on your X-ray, that's all. It doesn't mean you have anything. Don't jump to conclusions. *(Sighing)* Nothing's gonna happen to you. You're in the middle of New York City. This is your town. You're surrounded by people and traffic and restaurants.

Mickey brushes against a heavyset man who gives him a nasty look. Mickey is so dazed, he doesn't even notice.

MICKEY'S VOICE-OVER   I mean, God, how can you, how can you just one day . . . vanish? Keep calm. You're gonna be okay. Don't panic.

CUT TO:
INTERIOR. MICKEY'S APARTMENT/BEDROOM LOFT—NIGHT.

The dark bedroom is abruptly lit as Mickey, lying in his bed, wakes up with a start and turns on his night-table lamp.

MICKEY'S VOICE-OVER   I'm dying! I'm dying! I know it! There's a spot on my lungs! *(Sitting up, putting on his glasses)* All right now, take it easy, will you? It's not on your lungs. It's on your ear. No, it's the same thing, isn't it? *(Pulling the sheets off and sitting on the edge of his bed)* Oh, jeez, I can't sleep! Oh, God, there's a tumor in my head the size of a basketball! *(Putting on his slippers)* N-now I keep thinking I can feel it every time I blink! Oh, Jesus! He-he-he wants me to do a brain scan to confirm what he already suspects.
Mickey, still ruminating, stands up. Fixing his pants, he walks out of his bedroom loft into a dark upper hallway.

MICKEY'S VOICE-OVER *(Running his hand along a bannister)*   Look . . . I'll make a deal with God. Let it just be my ear, okay? I'll go deaf. I'll go deaf and blind in one eye maybe. But I don't want a brain operation! Once they go into my skull, I'll-I'll wind up like the guy with the, with the wool cap who delivers for the florist!
He walks down a spiral staircase into the dark living room.

MICKEY'S VOICE-OVER   Oh, relax, will ya? Your whole life you run to doctors. The news is always fine. *(Pausing at the bottom of the stairs)* That's not true. What about years ago?

The film cuts to a flashback of Mickey's past. Dr. Smith, sitting behind his desk, faces the camera. Rows of periodicals line the wall behind him.

DR. SMITH *(Gesturing with one hand)*   I'm sorry to say, Mr. Sachs, that you cannot have children.
The camera moves to Dr. Smith's point of view: Hannah and Mickey, sitting on the opposite side of the desk. They look stunned.

MICKEY *(Reacting, putting his hands across his chest)*   Gee.

HANNAH *(Reacting)*   Is there no chance?

DR. SMITH *(Getting up from his desk)*   Well, naturally, this doesn't mean that you can't have a normal sex life. *(Walking over to the opened office door and closing it)* But Mr. Sachs's tests indicate that he is infertile. Small sperm volume and infertile.
The camera moves back to the stunned Mickey and Hannah, following Dr. Smith with their eyes.

MICKEY *(Gesturing, looking up at an offscreen Dr. Smith)*   Isn't there anything I can do? Push-ups or hormones?

DR. SMITH *(Offscreen)*   I'm afraid not.

MICKEY   Well, I gotta get a second opinion.

HANNAH *(Turning to Mickey)*   This is the second opinion.

MICKEY *(Shrugging)*   Well, then a third opinion.
Dr. Smith walks back to his high-backed leather chair behind the desk and sits down. As he talks, the camera moves closer and closer to his face.

DR. SMITH   I realize this is a blow. My experience is that many very fine marriages become unstable and are destroyed by an inability to deal with this sort of problem. I hope you won't make too much of it. One can adopt children, and there are various artificial methods of fertilization.

CUT TO:
EXTERIOR. GROVE STREET IN GREENWICH VILLAGE—
DAY.

Mickey and Hannah walk on the sidewalk, oblivious of the passing
pedestrians. Hannah, crying, blows her nose.

MICKEY *(Gesturing)*   I'm so humiliated. I don't know what to say.
I mean—

HANNAH *(Interrupting, wiping her eyes with her tissue)*   Could you
have ruined yourself somehow?

MICKEY *(Gesturing)*   How could I ruin myself? What do you
mean, ruin myself?

HANNAH *(Overlapping, looking at Mickey)*   I don't know. Exces-
sive masturbation?

MICKEY   Hey, you gonna start knocking my hobbies? Jesus!
Hannah sobs, clutching her tissue to her face.

MICKEY   Maybe, maybe we can adopt a child. He said you could adopt one—

HANNAH *(Interrupting)*   Well, what about artificial insemination?

MICKEY *(Gesturing)*   What are you talking about?

HANNAH *(Overlapping)*   You know, where I-I-I would get implanted from a-a donor.

MICKEY *(Reacting)*   What, by a st-stranger?
Deep in conversation, they cross a tree-lined street. They pass a yellow wood-frame house bordered by a wrought-iron fence.

HANNAH   Yeah, they have these banks, you know, where they keep them frozen.

MICKEY *(Gesturing)*   Fro—? You want a-a defrosted kid? Is that your idea?

HANNAH   I want to experience childbirth.

MICKEY   With a, with a stranger? With a—

HANNAH *(Interrupting, sniffing)*   Just think about it. That's all I ask.
They walk offscreen and the film cuts to Hannah and Mickey's living room. The room is brightly lit; it's cluttered with pillows and plants. Norman and Carol, his wife, sit on the couch drinking coffee.

CAROL *(Putting down her cup)*   Oh, that was a wonderful show. I think that's the best show you two ever wrote.

NORMAN *(Holding his cup, pointing emphatically)*   No, the funniest show that Mickey and I ever did was the one we won the Emmy for.
Mickey walks from the kitchen into the living room, holding a half-eaten chocolate cake on a serving plate. The sun pours through the

windows he passes. Hannah is briefly seen in the background, preparing more coffee in the kitchen.

MICKEY   Yeah . . . I-I think as, I think as far as laughs, I mean just plain laughs, you know, that was probably the best thing that we ever did.
Mickey puts the cake down on the coffee table, which is already crowded with assorted plants, plates, and a bamboo tray holding utensils and napkins.

NORMAN *(Agreeing)*   Mm-hm.

CAROL *(Overlapping, her hands over her crossed knees and nodding)*   Yeah, it was funny, it was very funny. But the show was about the two Frenchmen, now that was funny and it was warm.
Mickey sighs and flops down on an adjoining couch. He rubs his forehead.

NORMAN *(To Carol, gesturing with his cup)*   We got that idea on that trip to Paris.

CAROL *(Nodding)*   Right.

NORMAN *(Smiling)*   Hmm?

CAROL *(To the offscreen Hannah)*   Do you remember that summer in France? Hannah, you had jet lag for six straight weeks.
Norman chuckles.

MICKEY *(Sighing, almost mumbling)*   Yeah, but it was, you know, I guess we had fun when we were there and, you know, it's just, I—

NORMAN *(Overlapping, nodding)*   Mm-hm.
Hannah walks over to the group, holding a pot of coffee. She awkwardly steps past Mickey to pour coffee for Norman and Carol.

HANNAH *(To Mickey)*   Sorry. *(To Norman and Carol)* Coffee? Listen, you guys, we were— You want some more?

NORMAN *(Holding out his cup)*   Mmm.

HANNAH *(Refilling Norman's cup)*   We-we . . . we had something we-we really wanted to discuss with you.

MICKEY *(Overlapping, coughing)*   Yeah . . .
Hannah refills Carol's cup. She puts the pot down on the coffee table and sits down next to Mickey.

MICKEY *(Standing up and gesturing)*   Jeez, this is, this is, this is very delicate and-and I only bring this up amongst friends, you know.
He starts to pace. Hannah, her hands clasped near her face, glances briefly at Carol.

MICKEY *(Turning to the group as he paces behind the couch)*   I mean . . . *(Grunting)* this is, uh . . . this should not go any further than this room.

NORMAN *(Sipping his coffee)*   I'm all ears.
Hannah sighs. Mickey pauses for a moment, collecting his thoughts.

MICKEY *(Gesturing and pacing)*   Hannah and I . . . can't have any children. Now I-I-I don't want to get into whose fault it— *(Gesturing)* It's my fault that we can't and-and-and the details are too embarrassing to—

HANNAH *(Interrupting, nervously picking at her fingers)*   W-w-we-we've decided after a lot of discussion that we-we'd try with artificial insemination.
Mickey stops his pacing and looks at the group.

MICKEY *(Putting his hands on his hips)*   Yeah, I'm not so sure that I, that I like that idea myself, anyway—
He starts to pace behind the couch anew.

HANNAH *(Overlapping)* Um, I-I didn't really want to, you know, go to a sperm bank or something, have some anonymous donor. *(Gesturing at Norman and Carol)* I-I just, you know, I-I-I wouldn't want that.

MICKEY *(Pacing)* Right. We felt that if we were gonna do it, that we would like somebody who we knew and who we liked and who was warm and bright and . . .
Norman and Carol remain silent.

HANNAH And you can say no . . . you know. Feel free to say no. W-we realize it has all kinds of implications.
Mickey stops pacing and leans on the couch behind Norman.

MICKEY Yeah, but the-the point that, uh, that we're making here is that we need some sperm.
Mickey, rubbing his hands on his knees, leans back against the wall. Norman and Carol turn to each other, reacting.

NORMAN *(Sighing)* Gee. *(Chuckling)* Well . . . My first reaction after the initial shock is, uh, flattered that you would ask me. *(Chuckling nervously)*
Carol glares at Norman.

MICKEY *(Pointing at himself)* Yeah, well, I would be the father. *(Pointing to Norman)* You would just have to masturbate into a little cup.

NORMAN *(Shrugging)* I can handle that.

HANNAH *(Scooting closer to Carol and Norman on the couch, gesturing)* Obviously we wou-wouldn't have intercourse.
She chuckles nervously.

CAROL *(To Hannah, chuckling nervously herself)* Gosh, listen. *(Rubbing her nose)* I've gotta tell you the truth here. I'm a little uneasy about this.

WOODY ALLEN

HANNAH *(Putting her hand on Carol's shoulder)* Carol, I know it's a lot to ask.

CAROL *(Gesturing)* Well . . . I feel for you. I do. I . . . I'm gonna cry. You want my husband to have a child with you?

HANNAH *(Gesturing)* Ye— D-d-d-don't answer now. Just, you know, take it home and think about it for a while.

NORMAN *(Holding his coffee cup, thoughtful)* I gave blood before and, uh . . . clothing to the poor.

CAROL *(To Norman, scratching her ear)* Okay, Norman, listen, I really want to talk about this at home. *(Nodding as Hannah looks briefly offscreen at Mickey)* I think it's a matter for your analyst . . . and mine.

NORMAN *(Emphatically)* And maybe my lawyer.
He takes a sip of coffee.

HANNAH *(Gesturing)* You know, we-we understand completely if, you know, if you feel you'd-you'd rather not. *(Chuckling nervously)* I didn't mean to spoil the evening. *(Rubbing her hands)* Now let's move on to another topic.
Hannah reaches for the cake as Carol and Norman exchange glances, reacting.

The flashback ends. Mickey is back in the present in his darkened living room, illuminated by a glow from a window behind the couch. A coffee table sits in front of the couch. Papers are scattered on the floor. Mickey gets up from the couch where he'd been sitting. He paces back and forth as he talks over the screen.

MICKEY'S VOICE-OVER So you had my ex-partner's baby. Twins. Maybe that did cause some trouble, but *(Sighing)* I think we were drifting apart anyhow. Now instead of man and wife we're just good friends. Boy, love is really unpredictable.

CUT TO:
INTERIOR. METROPOLITAN OPERA HOUSE—NIGHT.

Manon Lescaut *is being performed. Onstage, the soprano in the title role sings a mournful aria as she kneels by the ruins of a wagon. The background is dark. The film moves up to the private boxes in the upper loge. David and Holly can be seen from a distance sitting in one of the boxes. David glances at her; he reaches down for a bottle of wine. The movie briefly cuts back to the stage. The soprano is leaning on a wagon wheel; her voice soars. Then it's back to a closer look at Holly and David in their box. The aria continues as David hands a smiling Holly a glass. He uncorks the wine and pours some in both their glasses. Holly mouths a thank you, glancing around. They look at each other and raise their glasses in a toast.*

CUT TO:

Dusty bought this huge house in Southampton.

The opera audience is heard cheering, applauding, and sounding their "Bravos."

The clapping stops as the movie cuts to Frederick's loft. It is day. Lee, wearing a baggy plaid shirt and jeans, has opened the door for Elliot and his client, wealthy rock star Dusty Frye.

ELLIOT *(Leading the way into the loft, gesturing)* Lee, Frederick . . . say hello to Dusty Frye.
Lee closes the door behind the men and walks over to Dusty.

LEE *(Shaking Dusty's hand)* Hi, Dusty.

DUSTY Hi.
Lee chuckles as she looks at him; he is wearing sunglasses, a red-imprinted T-shirt, and a baggy coat. She turns and walks with Frederick, Elliot, and Dusty farther into the loft, her hands clasped behind her back.

ELLIOT *(As he walks)*   Dusty's just bought a huge house in Southampton and he's in the process of decorating it.

DUSTY   Yeah. It's kind of a weird place, actually. A lotta wall space. *(Chuckling)*

LEE   Oh.
They walk into the living room area of the loft, where Frederick, his hands in his pockets, neatly attired in vest sweater and white shirt, stands, waiting.

DUSTY *(To Frederick, giving him a "hip" handshake)*   How ya doin', man?

ELLIOT *(To a less than enthusiastic Frederick)*   I told him about your work, and he's very excited.

DUSTY   Yeah, I got an Andy Warhol. And I got a Frank Stella, too. Oh, it's very beautiful. *(Gesturing)* Big, weird . . . you know. *(Chuckling as he crosses his arms on his chest)* If you stare at that Stella too long, the colors just seem to float. It's kinda weird.
Frederick covers his face to hide his disgust.

LEE *(Chuckling, her arms crossed)*   Are you excited about becoming a collector?

DUSTY   Yeah.

LEE *(Nodding)*   Yeah?

DUSTY *(Shrugging)*   I got a lot more to learn, though. I really wasn't into art when I was a kid.

LEE *(Nodding)*   Uh-huh.

FREDERICK *(Addressing but not looking at Dusty)*   Do you appreciate drawings?

DUSTY *(Shrugging)*   Yeah. *(Chuckling as he notices and points to some offscreen drawings Frederick has set up)* Oh! Hey! Wow! *(Pointing to an offscreen nude drawing)* She's beautiful. But, uh, really, I-I-I-I need something . . . I'm looking for something big.
As Dusty talks, the camera follows Elliot, who walks past the others to examine the drawings more closely. Two framed nude drawings of Lee are propped up on an easel. Elliot glances admiringly at the drawings, then surreptitiously at Lee, admiring her body as she converses with an offscreen Dusty and Frederick.

LEE *(Looking at an offscreen Frederick, gesturing)*   Big. Frederick, show him the oils.

FREDERICK *(Offscreen)*   They're in the basement.
The camera leaves Elliot to follow the enthusiastic Lee as she takes Dusty by the arm and starts leading him to the door. Frederick follows at a distance.

LEE *(To Dusty)*   Frederick's done this whole new series that I'm sure you would really love.

DUSTY *(Overlapping, muttering)*   Well, are . . . are they big?

LEE   Yeah. Some of them . . . yeah, some of them are very big.

DUSTY   'Cause I got a lot of wall space there. *(Chuckling)*

FREDERICK *(Angrily stopping in his tracks)*   I don't sell my work by the yard!

LEE *(Chuckling, reacting)*   Oh, Frederick!
The camera now moves back to Elliot, still staring at the nude drawings, as the sounds of Frederick's and Dusty's footsteps are heard leaving the loft. He turns and hesitantly smiles to an offscreen Lee.

ELLIOT *(Chuckling softly)*   How's everything?

LEE *(Walking onscreen towards Elliot)*   Oh, you know . . . I talked to Hannah this morning on the phone, and she said that you two might be going to the country for the weekend.

ELLIOT   Yeah, she loves to go out in the woods.

LEE *(Nodding, her arms clasped around her chest)*   Oh, yeah.

ELLIOT *(Chuckling)*   But I go nuts. It's a conflict.
He laughs. Lee, uneasy, looks down.

LEE   I have to get my teeth cleaned this week.

ELLIOT   Oh, that's nice.
There's an awkward moment of silence.

ELLIOT *(Breaking the silence, pointing in the direction of the door)*   I
  figured I'd get, uh, Frederick and Dusty together.

LEE *(Looking in the same direction, gesturing)*   Oh, yeah, that's
  really nice of you.

ELLIOT   Yes. This kid, he's earned a trillion dollars.

LEE *(Nodding, wrapping her arms around her chest again)*   Oh.

ELLIOT   He's got like six gold records.

LEE *(Gesturing, relieved that she's found something to say)*   Oh,
  speaking of records . . . I bought that Mozart Trio you recommended . . .
  *The camera follows Lee as she walks quickly to the stereo unit, pulling
  a record off the shelf.*

LEE *(Continuing)*   . . . and the man in the record shop showed
  me another one that I think you'd love. It's a . . . another
  Bach, second movement.
  She pulls the record out of its jacket and puts it on the turntable.

ELLIOT *(Offscreen)*   Oh, you-you have that one?

LEE *(Working at the stereo, turning her head towards Elliot)*   Yeah.

ELLIOT *(Offscreen)*   Oh, I would love to hear it.

Bach's Concerto for Harpsichord fills the room.

LEE *(Putting the turntable cover in place)*   Oh, and Holly met a wonderful man who loves opera. An architect.

ELLIOT *(Offscreen)*   Oh, that's nice. I'd love to see her wind up settled. She's a tense one. *(Chuckling)*
The record in place, Lee turns and leans back against the stereo unit. She listens to the music, her eyes closed. The record plays for a few moments in the quiet room, as Elliot walks over to Lee and leans against the shelf near her.

LEE *(Intently)*   Isn't that beautiful?

ELLIOT *(Looking at Lee, his hands clasped in front of him)*   I know this. Bach. F Minor Concerto. It's one of my favorites.
Lee, smiling, continues to listen to the music, her head down; Elliot stares at her.

ELLIOT *(After a pause)*   Uh . . . did you ever get around to e. e. cummings?

LEE *(Wrapping her arms around her chest and looking away from Elliot for a moment)*   Yes, he's just adorable.
Elliot nods.

LEE *(Awkwardly)*   They have a very large gay clientele, you know, where I get my teeth cleaned, and . . . all the hygienists now wear gloves because they're afraid of AIDS.

ELLIOT *(Taking a breath)*   Oh, right.
There is another moment of silence. Elliot stares at Lee, who continues to look down, her arms around her chest. The harpsichord plays on.

ELLIOT *(Softly)*   Did you ever get around to the poem on page a hundred and twelve?

LEE   Yes, it made me cry *(Tentatively looking at Elliot)* it was so beautiful . . . so romantic.

Lee looks down again; the music plays softly and Elliot continues to stare at her, thinking.

ELLIOT'S VOICE-OVER   I want so badly to kiss her. Not here, you idiot. You've got to get her alone someplace.
As Elliot's thoughts are heard over the scene, Lee glances around the loft, then begins to walk away. The camera follows her as she goes past the nude drawings, which become the focus of attention as Lee walks offscreen.

ELLIOT'S VOICE-OVER   But I've got to proceed cautiously. This is a very delicate situation. Okay, uh . . . ask her if you can see her for lunch or a drink tomorrow.
Lee walks back onscreen, to the bookshelf behind the drawings. She takes the e. e. cummings book from the shelf and flips through it as she walks back to Elliot, who is still leaning by the stereo, still ruminating.

ELLIOT'S VOICE-OVER   And be ready to make light of the offer if she's unresponsive. This has to be done very skillfully, very diplomatically.

LEE *(Showing Elliot a poem in her book)*   Did you ever read this one—?
Elliot leaps up, grabs Lee, and kisses her passionately. Lee, surprised, pushes him away.

LEE   Elliot! Don't!

ELLIOT   Lee! Lee! Lee, I'm in love with you.
He kisses Lee again. He clumsily turns around; she bumps against the stereo unit. As Lee pulls away, she smashes into the turntable. The needle scratches loudly. Lee, shocked, is gasping. The record, pushed to a different part of the concerto, now plays a more complicated, faster fugue.

ELLIOT *(Breathing hard)*   Oh!

LEE *(Gasping)*   What are you doing?!

ELLIOT *(Frantically)*   I . . . I'm-I'm-I'm-I'm sorry. I have to talk
to you for . . . There's so much that I want to tell you.
Lee stares at Elliot in shock.

LEE *(Still gasping)*   Elliot!

ELLIOT *(Gesturing desperately)*   I have been in love with you for so
long.
Frederick and Dusty's indistinct voices, raised in argument, are sud-
denly heard. Elliot quickly turns away from Lee. She tries to compose
herself and the film cuts to the loft entranceway. Frederick enters the
loft first, followed by a confused Dusty. They stride across the loft past
Lee, who is standing by the stereo. Elliot, standing near the nude
drawings, is looking through a book.

FREDERICK *(Angrily)*   Please forget it! I don't have any interest
in selling anything!

DUSTY *(Gesturing)*   I ask you if you have something with a little
puce in it, you gotta fly off the handle!

LEE *(In a slightly higher-pitched voice)*   What's the problem?

FREDERICK *(Pulling the nude drawings off his easel angrily)*   I'm not
interested in what your interior decorator would think, okay?!

DUSTY *(Overlapping, gesturing)*   Well, I can't commit to anything
without consulting her first. That's what I have her for, okay?

FREDERICK *(Carrying the drawings off)*   This is degrading! You
don't buy paintings to blend in with the sofa!

DUSTY *(Looking after Frederick)*   It's not a sofa, it's an ottoman!
(Touching his forehead, turning to Elliot) God, forget it! Let's just
get outta here, Elliot.

ELLIOT *(Putting down the book)*   We'll go.

The film moves outside the loft building. Dusty and Elliot emerge and walk to Dusty's waiting limousine. Elliot is rubbing his forehead, anguished.

DUSTY *(Angrily, getting into the car)*   What a weirdo that guy is! Paranoid. *(Noticing Elliot's anguished face)* What's the matter with you?

ELLIOT *(Gesturing)*   Look I-I-I'll be okay. I'll be okay.

DUSTY *(Overlapping)*   It's not that big a deal. We just didn't hit it off.

ELLIOT *(Gesturing)*   Now, look, you-you-you go on ahead.

DUSTY   Are you okay? You look— You're sweatin'.

ELLIOT *(Overlapping, nervously)*   Yeah. Yeah, I just-just need so-some-some fresh air. It's probably something I ate. I'll-I'll walk. You go ahead.
Dusty settles down in the backseat and closes the door. Elliot leans down to the chauffeur's window, signaling for him to start driving.

ELLIOT *(Continuing, gesturing)*   You go. Go on. Go.
The limousine drives off. Elliot runs to a phone booth across the street. He picks up the phone and dials.

The films cuts to Frederick in his loft, standing near the phone. It rings. Frederick picks it up.

FREDERICK *(Into the telephone)*   Hello? Hello? Hello?
When no one answers, Frederick, reacting, hangs up, and the film moves back outside to the phone booth, where Elliot, the phone receiver to his ear, listens for a moment, then hangs up. He walks out of the booth, reacting, then walks down the sidewalk, where he bumps into a frantic Lee, just turning the corner.

LEE *(Gesturing in relief)*   Oh! There you are!
Elliot mumbles, relieved and confused.

LEE I was looking for you.

ELLIOT *(Gesturing)* I, I must apologize. I-I'm, I-I'm sorry. I'm so mixed up.

LEE *(Gesturing)* Well, how do you expect me to react to such a thing?
Elliot, uneasy, glances up in the direction of Frederick's loft. He leads Lee a few yards up the street, away from any prying eyes.

ELLIOT *(Taking Lee's arm)* Wh—, uh, I know, I know but, I am in love with you.

LEE Oh, don't say those words!

ELLIOT *(Overlapping, shaking his head)* I-I, I'm sorry. I know it's terrible.

LEE *(Pushing back her hair, shaking her head hopelessly)* Why, you know the situation.
She sighs.

ELLIOT *(Looking away for a moment)*   I know! I-I-I-I, I realize.

LEE   What do you expect me to say?

ELLIOT   Hannah and I are in the last stages.

LEE *(Shaking her head)*   Wh— She's never said anything, and we're very close. She'd tell me such a thing.

ELLIOT   Wh—, it-it-it-it, it's so sad. She's crazy about me, but somewhere on the, along the line, I've fallen out of love with her.

LEE   Not because of me, I hope.

ELLIOT   Oh, no, no. *(Nodding)* Well, yes! I love you.

LEE   Oh, I can't be the cause of anything between you and Hannah. I jus—

ELLIOT *(Overlapping, shaking his head)*   Oh, no, no, no. It, uh, it-it-it-it was i-inevitable that Hannah and I part, anyway.

LEE   Why?

ELLIOT   Tch, w-well, for a million reasons.

LEE *(Gesturing)*   But not over me?

ELLIOT   Tch, no! We were, we were both going in different directions.

LEE *(Looking down)*   Poor Hannah.

ELLIOT   But-but, but how about you? Do you, do you share any of my feelings? Or is this just an unpleasant embarrassment to you?

LEE *(Reacting uneasily)*   I can't say anything!

ELLIOT   W-well, please be candid. I, I-I don't want you to feel bad.

LEE *(Putting her hand to her head)* Yes! But I . . . I have certain
feelings for you, but don't make me say anything more, all
right?
Lee looks at him.

ELLIOT *(Gesturing)* O-o-o-okay, Lee. Okay, okay. You, you, y-
you've said enough. It's my responsibility now. I will work
things out.

LEE Look, don't do anything on my behalf. *(Shaking her head)* I
live with Frederick, and Hannah and I are close.

ELLIOT Yes, but you, you do care about me.

LEE *(Reacting)* Oh, Elliot, please! I can't be a party to this! I'm
suddenly wracked with guilt just standing here talking to you
on the street!
She sighs.

ELLIOT *(Emphatically)* Your guilt is because you feel the same.

LEE *(Reacting)* Oh, please, I have to go. I have to get my teeth
cleaned.
She walks off. Elliot stares after her, grinning.

ELLIOT *(Happily)* I have my answer. I have my answer! I'm
walking on air!
He laughs.

CUT TO:
*EXTERIOR. STREET CORNER OUTSIDE EVAN AND NOR-
MA'S APARTMENT BUILDING—DAY.*

*A taxi turns a West Side street corner and stops in front of Evan and
Norma's building, which is decorated with a long metal awning. It's
an overcast day. A station wagon on the opposite side of the street
pulls away as Hannah, a white scarf fluttering over her shoulder, gets*

out of the cab. She runs into the building; the taxi drives away. A piano plays "Bewitched" over the screen.

CUT TO:
INTERIOR. EVAN AND NORMA'S APARTMENT—DAY.

Evan, his back to the camera, walks to the front door and opens it to Hannah.

HANNAH *(Distracted)* Hi. How's she doing?

EVAN *(Overlapping)* I am glad to see you.
Hannah takes off her shoulder bag and her coat as her aggravated father walks past her towards the kitchen. He passes a wall with an ornate mirror and some framed photographs.

EVAN She's in the kitchen there. It's the same thing. Same thing. She promises, promises. *(Gesturing)* But it's all lies.
Through a doorway, Norma can be seen sitting on a chair in the kitchen. She wears a robe over a slip and stockings; she's drinking. Evan stands in the doorway looking at her; he doesn't go in.

HANNAH *(Offscreen, patiently)* Don't make it worse, Dad.

EVAN *(Overlapping)* Always.
Hannah hurriedly passes her father and enters the kitchen; her mother takes a sip of her drink.

HANNAH Hi, Mom. How you doing? Here, let me get you some coffee. That's enough of that. *(Taking away her mother's drink, to Evan)* What triggered it?

EVAN *(Gesturing, as Norma turns her head and watches him)* We were making a commercial down at the mayor's office, and there was this young, good-looking salesman . . .
Norma reacts, turning to her daughter. Hannah, however, has her back turned. She is busy taking charge in the kitchen as Evan speaks.

She takes some pills out of a cupboard and hands them to her mother with a glass of water.

EVAN *(Continuing)* . . . and your mother was throwing herself at him in a disgusting way, and when she found she was too old to seduce him, that he was just embarrassed by her—

NORMA *(Angrily interrupting, turning her head)* Liar! Liar!
The camera moves to Evan, who continues to tell his story, ignoring his wife's outburst, as he walks away from the kitchen doorway into the den.

EVAN Then at lunch she got drunker and drunker *(Shouting over his shoulder)* and finally she became Joan Collins!
Evan walks over to the piano, where several framed family photographs sit in a line on its top. He picks one up as Norma speaks offscreen in the kitchen.

NORMA *(Offscreen)* All my life I've had to put up with insults . . .

The camera moves back to the kitchen as Norma talks. She is still glaring offscreen at the doorway where Evan stood moments before. She holds the water glass and the pills.

NORMA *(Continuing dramatically)* . . . from this non-person, this, th-th-this haircut that passes for a man. *(Turning to look at the offscreen Hannah)* He could never support us. It's a good thing we had a talented daughter!
Evan is back in the doorway, listening to Norma, getting more and more angry. As he makes a retort, he starts to walk back to the den and his piano.

EVAN   I can only hope that she was mine. With you as her mother *(Gesturing, his voice getting louder)* her father could be anybody in Actors' Equity!

NORMA   She's talented . . . so it's not likely she's yours! *(Taking a sip of water)*

HANNAH *(Walking over to the doorway to speak to Evan, who's already fuming in the den)*   Dad, could you just please stay in the other room and let me take care of her?
Hannah goes back to Norma; she takes the glass of water away.

EVAN *(Offscreen, choosing to ignore Hannah's suggestion)*   You never know when she's going to fall off the wagon and humiliate everybody.
Hannah, choosing to ignore Evan's remark, hands her mother a cup of coffee; she puts her mother's hands on the cup.

HANNAH   Here, Mom. Drink this. *(Leaning against a kitchen counter)* You know, you're awful. You probably were flirting.

NORMA *(Sipping her coffee)*   No! I like to joke around and have fun, and he gets angry because I get the attention. He's gotten sourer as he's gotten older, and I've tried to stay young . . . at heart.

HANNAH   You promised to stay on the wagon.

NORMA *(Shaking her head)*   The sacrifices I've made because of that man. *(Inhaling)* He's ruined me with his ego, his philandering, his— *(Gesturing)* his-his-his-his mediocrity!

HANNAH   Okay, stop being so dramatic.

NORMA *(Shouting to the offscreen Evan)*   He's the one that's made every ingenue in stock!

HANNAH *(Quietly)*   Okay, okay.

NORMA *(Touching Hannah's arm, gasping)*   Th-th-they, they wanted me for a screen test.

HANNAH *(Patiently)*   Yeah, I know, Mom.

NORMA *(Gesturing)*   But I, I knew that he'd get up there and he'd flounder around with his expensive haircuts and hairdos and clothes. He's all show! *(Touching Hannah's arm again, then touching her chest)* Now how can you act when there's nothing inside to come out?!
Norma sips her coffee, softly sobbing. Hannah, reacting, walks away from the counter and, capping the bottle of pills, puts them back in the cupboard. Evan plays the piano offscreen. The camera moves in on Hannah's face as she reflects, her voice heard over the screen.

HANNAH'S VOICE-OVER   She was so beautiful at one time, and he was so dashing. Both of them just full of promise and hopes that never materialized.
The camera leaves Hannah's face as she continues to reflect; it moves to the den, to the row of family photos on the piano: one of a present-day Evan and Norma, others where both Norma and Evan are young, beautiful, hopeful. The music plays on.

HANNAH'S VOICE-OVER   And the fights and the constant infidelities to prove themselves . . . and blaming each other. It's s-sad. They loved the idea of having us kids, but raising us didn't interest them much. But it's impossible to hold it against them. They didn't know anything else.
The film cuts back to the kitchen. Norma stands up; Hannah takes her coffee cup and sets it on the counter.

NORMA   You know, of all of us in the family, you were the one blessed with the true gift.
She puts her arm around Hannah's shoulder. Mother and daughter walk out of the kitchen.

HANNAH *(Holding the hand her mother had placed on her shoulder)*   Ohhh, my true gift is luck, Mom.
Norma chuckles.

HANNAH *(Overlapping)*   I just had a lot of luck . . . from my first show, you know? I've always thought Lee was the one destined for great things.

NORMA   Yes, she's lovely, but she doesn't have your spark. *(Gesturing and chuckling)* She knows it. She worships you. She wouldn't dare get up there on the stage.

HANNAH *(Looking at her mother)*   Now, Holly's not shy.
They stop at the entrance to the den. Evan can be seen playing the piano as they continue their conversation.

NORMA   No, Holly's game for anything. Holly takes after me.

HANNAH   True.

NORMA *(Shaking her head)*   I'd have been a great dope addict.
Norma chortles. Hannah laughs, touching her mother. They walk over to Evan at the piano.

EVAN *(Looking up)* Remember this, Hannah?
Evan plays a few bars of "You Are Too Beautiful" as mother and daughter, their backs to the camera, listen. Norma leans over the piano; Hannah looks off into the distance, deep in reflection. The piano music continues in the background as the movie cuts to:

Lee walking along a wharf by the waterfront. The wind blows her hair; she hugs the e. e. cummings book to her chest. She, too, is deep in thought. She stops at the edge of the wharf; the camera continues to move, to a group of wooden pilings nearby, lapped by the water.

CUT TO:

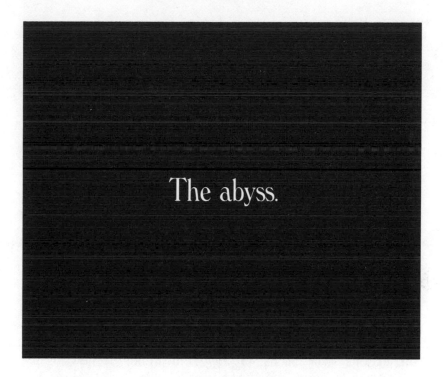

The piano piece ends and the film is quiet.

CUT TO:
INTERIOR. HOSPITAL CAT-SCAN ROOM—DAY.

The quiet continues as the film cuts to a close-up of a large, circular CAT-scan module in an antiseptic hospital room. A slowly moving stretcher, bearing Mickey's strapped prone body, begins to enter the round opening of the module. As the camera pulls back from Mickey, his taped head under the scan, two technicians can be seen through the window separating the scanner from the control room. One of them, sitting down, taps information into a computer while the other technician stands nearby, looking from Mickey to the computer screen.

The movie then cuts briefly to the computer screen, showing an image of Mickey's skull. Scan lines bleep over the skull. The camera moves up from the screen to reveal Mickey once again, as seen through the window, silent and serious under the CAT-scan module.

From Mickey's prone form, the film moves to the two technicians, as seen through the window in the scanner room. They examine the computer screen and talk indistinctly to each other. One of the men, nodding, taps more information into the computer.

While they're studying the CAT-scan picture, the camera cuts to a back view of Mickey under the module. There is a science-fiction feel to this scene, as if Mickey is lying in the center of a huge, white, futuristic circle. The stretcher, bearing Mickey, slowly moves out of the module.

CUT TO:
INTERIOR. DR. BROOKS'S OFFICE—DAY.

Dr. Brooks, holding Mickey's X-rays, walks past a row of bookshelves to his light panel. He props up the X-rays.

DR. BROOKS   Mr. Sachs, *(Sighing)* I'm afraid the news is not good.
Dr. Brooks turns to an offscreen Mickey.

DR. BROOKS *(Continuing, taking a pencil out of his pocket)*   If I can show you exactly where the tumor is, and why we feel that surgery would be of no use.
The film quickly cuts to a close-up of Mickey's face, reacting in total despair. He closes his eyes; he covers his face with his hand.

MICKEY'S VOICE-OVER   It's over. I'm face-to-face with eternity.

DR. BROOKS *(Offscreen)*   . . . grown quite large without being detected . . . *(Trailing off indistinctly as Mickey continues his anguished ramblings)*

MICKEY'S VOICE-OVER   Not later, but now. I'm so frightened I can't move, speak, or breathe.

HANNAH AND HER SISTERS

As Mickey finishes his speech, the "real" Dr. Brooks is seen walking into the office. The previous scene had been a figment of Mickey's imagination, a nightmare fantasy only. Holding Mickey's X-rays, the "real" Dr. Brooks walks past the same row of books to the light panel.

DR. BROOKS   Well, you're just fine. There's absolutely nothing here at all. And your tests are all fine. *(Switching on the light on the panel and propping up the X-rays)* I must admit, I was concerned, given your symptoms. *(Turning to look at the offscreen Mickey)* What caused this hearing loss in one ear, I guess we'll never really know for sure. But whatever it was, it's certainly not anything serious at all. *(Nodding)* I'm very relieved.

CUT TO:

The exterior of Mount Sinai Hospital. Once again, Mickey is seen leaving the building, but this time he bounds down the steps, jumping for joy. He runs swirling down the street, clapping his hands, happy with relief. Upbeat, uptempo jazz plays in the background. Several cars pass as Mickey joyfully runs. Suddenly he stops, his hand to his mouth, reflecting.

CUT TO:
INTERIOR. MICKEY'S OFFICE—DAY.

Gail sits in a chair in front of a bookshelf. A sofa, a coffee table holding periodicals, and an endtable with a lamp complete the tableau. Gail's hands are clasped on her lap.

GAIL   What do you mean you're quitting? Why? The news is good! You don't have canc—the thing.
Mickey, standing behind his desk, his back to the camera, his coat still on, looks out at the Manhattan skyline.

MICKEY   Do you realize what a thread we're all hanging by?

GAIL *(Offscreen)*   Mickey, you're off the hook. You should be celebrating.

MICKEY *(Walking around to the front of his desk, gesturing)*   Can you understand how meaningless everything is? Everything! I'm talking about nnnn— our lives, the show . . . the whole world, it's meaningless.

GAIL *(Gesturing)*   Yeah . . . but you're not dying!

MICKEY   No, I'm not dying *now*, but, but *(Gesturing)* you know, when I ran out of the hospital, I, I was so thrilled because they told me I was going to be all right. And I'm running down the street, and suddenly I stop, 'cause it hit me, all right, so, you know, I'm not going to go today. I'm okay. I'm not going to go tomorrow. *(Pointing)* But eventually, I'm going to be in that position.
Gail gets up from her chair. She walks past Mickey to a nearby cabinet. She opens a drawer, rummaging around for something. The camera follows her, leaving Mickey briefly.

GAIL   You're just realizing this now?

MICKEY *(Offscreen)*   Well, I don't realize it now, I know it all the time, but, but I managed to stick it in the back of my mind . . .
As Mickey continues to talk offscreen, Gail closes the cabinet drawer and walks to a file cabinet behind Mickey's desk.

MICKEY   . . . because it-it's a very horrible thing to . . . think about!
Gail opens the file cabinet and takes out a pack of gum. She slams it closed, distracted.

GAIL *(Muttering)*   Yeah. What?

MICKEY *(Turning to Gail)*   Can I tell you something? Can I tell you a secret?

GAIL *(Nodding impatiently as she walks around the desk)*   Yes, please.

HANNAH AND HER SISTERS

MICKEY *(Pointing)*   A week ago, I bought a rifle.

GAIL *(Sitting on the arm of a chair near Mickey)*   No.

MICKEY *(Overlapping, nodding and gesturing)*   I went into a store, I bought a rifle. I was gonna . . . You know, if they told me that I had a tumor, I was going to kill myself. The only thing that mighta stopped me, *might've,* is my parents would be devastated. I would, I woulda had to shoot them, also, first. And then, I have an aunt and uncle, I would have . . . You know, it would have been a bloodbath.

GAIL *(Shrugging, unwrapping a stick of gum)*   Tch, well, you know, eventually it, it is going to happen to all of us.

MICKEY   Yes, but doesn't that ruin everything for you? That makes everything . . .
Gail sighs. She pops a piece of gum into her mouth as Mickey continues to speak.

MICKEY *(Continuing)*   . . . you know it, it just takes the pleasure out of everything. *(Gesturing, pointing)* I mean, you're gonna

die, I'm gonna die, the audience is gonna die, the network's gonna— The sponsor. Everything!

GAIL *(Chewing)*   I know, I know, and your hamster.

MICKEY *(Nodding emphatically)*   Yes!

GAIL *(Chewing and pointing to Mickey)*   Listen, kid, I think you snapped your cap.
Mickey sighs.

GAIL *(Continuing, chewing loudly)*   Maybe you need a few weeks in Bermuda, or something. Or go to a whorehouse! No?

MICKEY *(Shaking his head, his hand to his chest)*   I can't stay on this show. I gotta get some answers. Otherwise *(Pausing and holding his head)* I'm telling you, I'm going to do something drastic.

CUT TO:

The entrance to the St. Regis Hotel, elegant and warmly lit in the night. Pedestrians pass. Baroque harpsichord music plays over the scene. The camera moves up the hotel's façade, past its welcoming flags, to its ornate windows several floors up.

As the harpsichord continues to play, the film moves inside, to one of the hotel rooms. Elliot, his back to the camera, is opening the door to Lee.

Elliot closes the door behind her as she enters. They stand very close to each other, framed by the door and a stark, subtly striped wallpapered wall.

ELLIOT *(Looking intensely at Lee, his hands in his pockets)*   I thought you weren't coming.

LEE   I almost didn't.

ELLIOT *(Putting his hand on her shoulder, wanting to kiss her)*   Lee . . . Uh . . .

HANNAH AND HER SISTERS

LEE   I didn't sleep all night.

ELLIOT *(Taking his hand away, gesturing to the room)*   No, no-no-no, I'm sure.
They walk towards the camera, further into the room. Elliot puts his arm around Lee.

LEE   What are we doing, meeting in a hotel room? It's terrible, isn't it?
The music stops. The camera follows Lee as she walks towards the curtained windows, past a fireplace, a mirror, some innocuous pictures, a delicate table holding a lamp, the foot of the bed.

ELLIOT *(Offscreen)*   I-I couldn't think where to invite you without taking risks.

LEE   I promised myself I wouldn't let this happen till you were living alone. I was so torn when you called.
She parts a corner of the curtains, looking out the window, turning when Elliot speaks.

ELLIOT *(Offscreen)*   I've wanted to call you everyday since I first told you how I felt.
He walks over to Lee by the curtained windows.

ELLIOT   I resisted so many times. *(Pausing)* Don't think badly of me.
He takes Lee into his arms.

ELLIOT   This is not an easy situation.

LEE *(Whispering)*   I know it isn't.
They kiss, their figures almost silhouetted in the warm glow of the room. Elliot takes Lee's coat off without breaking the kiss. They embrace. They kiss each other lightly, then stronger, more passionately, their embrace much tighter.

And it's later that night. The harpsichord music begins to play again as the camera moves over the bed covers to reveal Lee, lying content-

edly under the sheets, her hair fanned out on the pillows, one arm near her head.

LEE   That was just perfect. You've ruined me for anyone else.

ELLIOT *(Offscreen)*   I don't want anyone else ever to have you.

LEE *(Sighing)*   I was so worried I wouldn't compare with Hannah.

ELLIOT *(Offscreen, laughing)*   Oh, my God.
He enters the screen, sitting down on the edge of the bed next to Lee. He holds a cigarette.

ELLIOT   You really do have those thoughts, don't you?

LEE *(Chuckling, touching Elliot's arm)*   Oh, all the time.
Elliot chuckles; they hold hands.

LEE   I know she must be a really passionate person.

ELLIOT *(Looking at their clasped hands)*   Yes, she's, she's very warm, but, but it-it's me that wants to be giving to you. I-I-I want to do things for you. Hannah doesn't need me as much. *(Chuckling as Lee laughs)* I'm being presumptuous. Not that you *need* me.

LEE *(Nodding)*   I want you to take care of me . . . And I love when you do things to me.
Elliot leans down to Lee; they begin to kiss passionately.

CUT TO:
EXTERIOR. STREET OUTSIDE FREDERICK'S LOFT— NIGHT.

Lee walks along the sidewalk in the rain; she's bareheaded. The streets are dark. A car drives by; a pedestrian passes holding an umbrella. Lee passes a restaurant well lit inside by hanging lamps. The baroque music continues as she enters the loft, her head soaked. She closes the door, touching her soaking hair.

FREDERICK *(Offscreen)* You're late.
Lee walks through the loft's living room area, unbelting her coat, towards the bathroom. She passes Frederick, who sits at a table in the kitchen area, drinking a cup of coffee and reading the paper. A plate with a half-eaten sandwich sits in front of him. The music stops.

LEE *(Opening the bathroom door)* Lucy and I kept talking, and I didn't realize how late it had gotten.

FREDERICK *(Barely glancing up from his paper)* You missed a very dull TV show about Auschwitz. More gruesome film clips . . . and more puzzled intellectuals declaring their mystification over the systematic murder of millions.
As he talks, Lee is seen turning on the bathroom light. She takes off her coat, hanging it on a hook, then begins to dry her hair with a towel.

FREDERICK *(Turning his head slightly in Lee's direction and gesturing)* The reason why they could never answer the question "How could it possibly happen?" is that it's the wrong question. Given what people are, the question is *(Swallowing)* "Why doesn't it happen more often?" Of course it does, in subtler forms.
Frederick takes a bite of his sandwich and another sip of coffee as Lee walks out of the bathroom, tossing the towel down on the counter.

LEE *(Moving her fingers through her wet hair)* I have a little headache from this weather.
She takes a kettle and fills it with water.

FREDERICK *(Grunting, sipping his coffee)* It's been ages since I sat in front of the TV . . . just changing channels to find something.
As Frederick continues his monologue, Lee is busy in the background:

striking a wooden match and lighting a burner on the stove for the kettle, taking a glass out of the cupboard, walking into the bathroom for some pills, filling the glass with water in the kitchen sink, and taking her pills.

FREDERICK   You see the whole culture . . . Nazis, deodorant salesmen, wrestlers . . . beauty contests, the talk show . . . Can you imagine the level of a mind that watches wrestling? *(Gesturing)* Hmm? But the worst are the fundamentalist preachers . . . third-rate con men, telling the poor suckers that watch them that they speak for Jesus . . . and to please send in money. *(Picking up his sandwich)* Money, money, money! If Jesus came back, and saw what's going on in his name, he'd never stop throwing up.
He takes a bite of his sandwich and a sip of coffee. Lee sets her glass on the kitchen counter and walks towards the bedroom area.

LEE   *(Impatiently, her hands in her hair)*   Oh, God, Frederick, could you please lighten up?! I'm really not in the mood to hear a review of contemporary society again.

She starts to take off her wet clothes by the bed. Frederick takes off his glasses. He turns and looks at Lee in surprise.

FREDERICK *(Standing up from the table)* You know, you've been very nervous lately.

LEE *(Sighing)* I can't take this anymore.

FREDERICK *(Walking over to the bed)* I'm just trying to complete an education I started on you five years ago.

LEE *(Unbuttoning her blouse)* I'm not your pupil. *(Sighing, her hands at her side)* I was, but I'm not.

FREDERICK *(Sitting down on the edge of the bed)* When you leave the nest, I just want you to be ready to face the real world. *He pulls Lee down next to him on the bed.*

LEE *(Putting her hand on Frederick's leg)* Frederick, we're going to have to make some changes. *She sighs.*

FREDERICK *(Quickly looking at Lee, alarmed)* Like what?

LEE Oh, you know what. I'm suffocating!

FREDERICK *(Turning away, his hands clasped in front of him)* Oh! Are we going to have this conversation again?

LEE Yes, we're going to have this conversation again. I . . . I have to leave. I have to move out.

FREDERICK *(Shaking his clasped hands intensely)* Why?

LEE *(Sighing)* Because I have to!

FREDERICK *(Emotionally)* What are you going to use for money?!

LEE I don't know. I thought, maybe I'd move in with my parents for a while.

FREDERICK   Tch, oh. I always told you you would leave me. *(Looking at Lee)* But . . . does it have to be now?

LEE *(Hugging her arm with her other hand)*   Well, maybe it'll only be temporary, but I ha— I have to try.

FREDERICK *(Taking Lee's head in his hands and looking at her)*   Oh . . . Lee, you are my whole world. *(Pausing)* Good God! Have you been kissed tonight?!

LEE *(Reacting, pushing Frederick's hands from her face)*   No.

FREDERICK *(Reacting)*   Oh, yes, you have!

LEE *(Quickly standing up, defensively)*   No.

FREDERICK *(Raising his voice)*   You've been with someone!

LEE *(Overlapping, running away from the bed)*   Stop accusing me!
Lee runs into the kitchen, her hands tight around her chest.

FREDERICK *(Offscreen)*   I'm too smart, Lee! You can't fool me! You're turning all red!
Lee, fraught with emotion, briefly puts her outstretched hands on the refrigerator door, then turns around and leans against it, hugging herself, her blouse still unbuttoned, her hair still wet and bedraggled.

LEE   Leave me alone!
Frederick enters the kitchen area and leans against the counter.

FREDERICK *(Angrily)*   Oh, Christ! What's wrong with you?!

LEE *(Leaning against the refrigerator, sighing)*   I'm sorry.

FREDERICK   Oh, couldn't you say something? You have to slither around behind my back!

LEE *(Overlapping, her voice emotionally raised)*   I'm saying it now!

FREDERICK   So you met somebody else?

LEE *(Sighing, nodding)* Yeah.
Frederick cringes, reacting. He puts his hand to his forehead; he sighs.

LEE *(Walking into the bathroom)* But you, God, you knew that was going to happen sooner or later. I can't live like this!

FREDERICK *(Turning to face Lee in the bathroom, his arms crossed)* Who is it?

LEE *(Frantically putting things in her purse, glaring at Frederick)* What's the difference?! It's just somebody I met!

FREDERICK But who? Where did you meet him?

LEE It doesn't make a difference! I have to move out!

FREDERICK You are, you are my only connection to the world!
Lee turns and faces Frederick in the bathroom doorway.

LEE *(Gesturing emotionally)* Oh, God, that's too much responsibility for me. It's not fair! I want a less complicated life, Frederick. I want a husband, maybe even a child before it's too late.

FREDERICK *(Reacting, his face in his hand)* Jesus . . . Jesus!

LEE *(Gesturing, moving closer to Frederick)* Oh, God, I don't even know what I want.

FREDERICK *(Sighing heavily, reacting)* Oh . . .

LEE *(Rubbing Frederick's shoulder tenderly)* Tch, oh, what do you get out of me, anyway? I mean . . . *(Laying her head against his shoulder, sighing deeply)* it's not sexual anymore. It's certainly not intellectual. I mean, you're so superior to me in every way that—
Frederick furiously shakes Lee away. He pounds his fist against a cupboard. Lee, gasping, moves away.

FREDERICK Please, don't patronize me!
He puts his hand on his forehead, then turns to the offscreen Lee.

FREDERICK God! I should have married you years ago when you wanted to! I should have agreed.
He walks over to Lee in another area of the kitchen.

LEE *(Sighing)* Oh, God, don't you know it never would have worked?
Frederick turns away from Lee. He begins to pace near the counter.

FREDERICK I told you, one day you would leave me . . . *(Leaning on the counter)* for a younger man. I—
He loudly pounds his fist on the counter in despair and frustration, then covers his eyes with his hands in sorrow.

CUT TO:
INTERIOR. HANNAH'S BEDROOM—NIGHT.

Hannah, wearing a plaid shirt, sits up in bed, a book propped up on her knees. A cupboard with some bric-a-brac is mounted behind the night table, which holds a small, white, warm-glowing lamp and some photographs. She turns the page as Elliot, in pajamas and silk bathrobe, enters. She continues to read her book as he sits down at the edge of the bed and muses. His voice is heard over the screen.

ELLIOT'S VOICE-OVER What passion today with Lee. She's a volcano. It was a totally fulfilling experience . . . Just as I dreamed it would be. *(Nodding slightly as he takes off his slippers)* That's what it was. It was like living out a dream . . . a great dream. *(Taking off his bathrobe)* Now I feel very good and cozy being here next to Hannah. There's something very lovely and real about Hannah. *(Tossing his bathrobe aside and lying down on the bed next to Hannah, his hands crossed over his stomach)* She gives me a very deep feeling of being part of something. She's a wonderful woman . . . and I betrayed her. She came into my empty life and changed it . . . and I paid her back by banging her sister in a hotel room. God, I'm despicable. What a cruel and shallow thing to do. *(Sitting up)* I have to call her

now and tell her what we did was crazy. *(Anxiously)* It can't ever happen again. I'm not that kind of man . . . and I value Hannah too much. I love my wife. Now I've betrayed her. Oh, God!
Elliot frantically stands up and leaves the room.

HANNAH *(Reading, not looking up)*   Where're you going?

ELLIOT *(Offscreen)*   I've, uh . . . gotta find, gotta get a phone number in my desk. I forgot to phone Mel Kaufman.

HANNAH *(Still reading)*   It's so late.

ELLIOT *(Offscreen)*   Yeah, I know. I-I can't believe I forgot.
Elliot walks quickly into the darkened hallway.

ELLIOT *(Muttering)*   What if he answers? *(Turning into the doorway leading to the living room)* I'll hang up. *(Walking into the darkened living room)* I'll tell her we can't communicate until I terminate my marriage. *(Whispering)* It's immoral.
Elliot switches on the light. He paces back and forth in front of the piano and an accompanying music stand. The top of the piano is filled with family photos; the lamp he turned on illuminates some framed pictures on the wall and the piece of sheet music open on the piano.

ELLIOT *(Gesturing and whispering)*   Then, time will pass. I won't call, and she'll get the idea. I gotta stop this before I get in too deep. I'd rather hurt Lee a little, than destroy Hannah.
Elliot stops pacing and checks his wristwatch.

ELLIOT *(Whispering, rubbing his hands)*   It's one-thirty. She . . . she can't have a conversation with me . . . with him around. I'm getting hysterical. *(Putting his hands on his hips)* I'll call her first thing in the morning. I'll call her at six. *(Pointing)* Frederick goes jogging at six, yeah, she'll be alone. And I'll, I'll call her and nip it in the bud.
The phone rings. Elliot jumps.

ELLIOT *(Loudly, to the offscreen Hannah, gasping)* I've got it! I've got it! I've got it! *(Picking up the phone, into the telephone)* Hello? *(Loudly, for the offscreen Hannah's benefit)* Mel!
The movie cuts to Lee, standing in the dark in Frederick's loft. She talks softly into the telephone.

LEE *(Into the telephone)* I would have hung up if you hadn't answered and I promise I won't ever do this again, but I just had to tell you, I feel very close to you tonight. Very, very close. *(Pausing)* Good night.
Lee hangs up the phone and the movie cuts back to Elliot, standing in his living room. Stunned, he slowly lowers the phone receiver.

CUT TO:

"The only absolute knowledge attainable by man is that life is meaningless." —Tolstoy

Jazz is heard as the movie cuts to the outside of a university library, the camera focused on a huge replica of Rodin's Thinker *before moving to the front entrance. Mickey can be seen emerging from its depths. He wears his raincoat, his hands are in his pockets. He ponders the scene as he walks past the statue and a small front garden and down the sidewalk. Passersby, some holding books, are seen.*

MICKEY'S VOICE-OVER   Millions of books written on every conceivable subject by all these great minds, and, and in the end, none of 'em knows anything more about the big questions of life than I do. Ss— I read Socrates. You know, n-n-n—, this guy used to kn-knock off little Greek boys. What the hell's he got to teach me? And, and Nietzsche with his, with his Theory of Eternal Recurrence. He said that the life we live, we're gonna live over and over again the exact same way for eternity. Great. That means I, uh, I'll have to sit through the Ice Capades again. Tch. It's not worth it.
The movie next cuts to a sunny day in Central Park. A male jogger, seen through some tree branches, runs by. The camera moves past him, revealing a pondering Mickey walking by the reservoir. He continues to talk over the screen.

MICKEY'S VOICE-OVER   And, and Freud, another great pessimist. Jeez, I was in analysis for years. Nothing happened. My poor analyst got so frustrated. The guy finally put in a salad bar.
Several joggers pass Mickey; he continues to ruminate.

MICKEY'S VOICE-OVER   Oh! Look at all these people jogging . . . trying to stave off the inevitable decay of the body. Boy *(Smacking his lips)* it's so sad what people go through with their-their stationary bike and their exercise and their . . . *(Glancing at a fat woman jogger in a red sweatsuit who runs by)* . . . Oh! Look at this one! Poor thing. My God, she has to tote all that fat around. Maybe the poets are right. Maybe love is the only answer.

Mickey goes over to the chain-link fence encircling the reservoir. He stops walking and looks out over the water.

MICKEY'S VOICE-OVER   Shh— Of course, I was in love with Hannah. That didn't work out too well. *(Sighing)* I even took her sister out. Remember that?
Mickey continues to look through the fence at the water and the distant skyline. A jogger crosses in front of him. It's very quiet; the soft jazz continues.

MICKEY'S VOICE-OVER   Remember years ago when Hannah and I got divorced and she fixed me up with her sister Holly?
The film cuts abruptly to Mickey's flashback of his date with Holly, beginning with a rock club performance. The soft jazz becomes loud, pulsating rock. Three punkers—a girl with pink hair, a girl with a spiked mohawk, and a guy with Stevie Wonder braids and sunglasses —watch and bop their heads to the sounds of the offscreen rock band, The 39 Steps.

The camera moves to the stage, revealing a sleazy-looking rock band in the midst of their number.

THE 39 STEPS *(Singing)*   "I want to be like you / I said I'm going to fit into your group . . ."
As the band loudly plays on, the camera moves across the spellbound audience, sitting at crowded, smoky, small tables, to reveal a stricken Mickey and a mesmerized Holly squeezed together at one of them. A nearby member of the audience swills beer from a bottle. Holly, beating time to the music and enjoying herself, takes a puff of her cigarette. She wears a wristful of silver bracelets. She glances at Mickey impatiently. He's the only one in the place wearing a suit.

THE 39 STEPS *(Singing)*   "I don't wanna be different / Said I'm gonna be just like you / Because I'm gonna buy the records / That they play on radio . . ."
Holly turns back to the band, who are still in full swing. The camera

moves down the body of the lead singer, singing into a microphone, from his longish, curly red hair, through his cut-off red shirt and sweaty torso, to his guitar. He wears several silver bracelets on his wrists and gold bracelets on his upper arm. The microphone screeches feedback.

THE 39 STEPS *(Singing)* "I'm gonna dance at clubs / Gonna do just what I'm told / Because I'm bleedin' now / And I'm bleedin' now / I wanna slip, slip, slip, slip, slip / Into the crowd / I wanna slip, slip, slip, slip, slip / Into the crowd . . ."
The camera moves back to Holly and the even more stricken-looking Mickey. They are crowded in with people. In the background, a waitress holds up a tray. A man drinks from a glass mug; people chatter indistinctly over the loud band. The club is noisy, smoky, and thick with people. Holly glances at Mickey once again, this time unable to contain her annoyance.

HOLLY   Oh, why are you making those faces?

MICKEY *(Leaning over to Holly, gesturing)*   I can't hear you. I can't hear anything. I'm, I'm, I'm, I'm gonna lose hearing in my ear! I'm—

HOLLY *(Interrupting, gesturing to the offscreen band)*   Listen, you are witnessing genius!

MICKEY *(Pointing to his ears)*   I, I, my ears are experiencing a meltdown! I can't hear anything.

HOLLY *(Overlapping, gesturing dramatically)*   Look, can't you feel the energy? It's tangible energy! The room's alive with positive vibrations!
She opens a vial of cocaine.

MICKEY *(Gesturing, trying to talk over the band)*   Holly, I'm

frightened! I'm— After they sing . . . they're gonna take hostages! Now let's—
Holly holds a short metal straw of cocaine to her nose and sniffs it.

MICKEY *(Panicking)* Don't, no, please. Will you— No, don't . . .

HOLLY *(Holding the straw towards Mickey)* You want some?

THE 39 STEPS *(Singing in the background while Holly and Mickey talk)* "I want to dress like you / Say, I'll buy all the clothes / I want to fuck like you / Yeah, I'm sure it shows / Because I'm . . ."

MICKEY *(Shaking his head)* I don't. No. No.

HOLLY *(Overlapping, sniffing)* Come on, Mickey. Come on.

MICKEY *(Overlapping, gesturing)* But, no, you've been doing that all night! You're gonna . . . you're gonna burn a hole in your . . . You're gonna develop a third nostril! Really, *(Putting his hand on Holly's shoulder)* don't, please.
While Mickey pleads with her, Holly puts her cocaine vial into her purse. She holds a finger against one nostril and sniffs. She then picks up her lit cigarette and continues to smoke.

MICKEY Can we, can we go?

HOLLY *(Looking at the offscreen band, bopping her head to the music and smoking)* No!

MICKEY *(Touching his ear in pain)* My—uh . . .
The camera leaves the crowded tables and moves back to the band. The lead singer continues to sing with his band, swaying his body to the music . . .

THE 39 STEPS *(Singing)* ". . . Gonna buy the records / That they play on the radio . . ."

. . . as the film cuts abruptly to outside the rock club. The music has stopped. Mickey and Holly, almost in dark silhouette, are walking at a fast clip along the sidewalk, arguing. They pass some lighted clothing store windows; a few cars go by in the dark street.

HOLLY *(Enthusiastically)*   I love songs about extraterrestrial life, don't you?

MICKEY   Not when they're sung by extraterrestrials.

HOLLY *(Impatiently, with annoyance)*   Oh, well, I cannot communicate with you! I, you know, I never realized you were such a tightass.

MICKEY   I can't understand you. Your sisters, both sisters have such good taste in music. I don't know where you went, went wrong.

HOLLY *(Gesturing)*   Do you mind? I'm-I'm my own person.

MICKEY   Can I take you someplace to hear something nice?

HOLLY *(Touching the hat on her head)*   Eh, Mickey, it's getting late.

MICKEY   Now come on, you're be—, 'cause you're being angry at me.
They stop briefly at a street corner and look for oncoming cars before crossing. Mickey takes Holly's arm as they walk across the street towards the camera.

HOLLY *(Angrily)*   I'm not angry! You know, you, well, you don't believe in ESP, you don't like rock music, you won't get high . . . It's like I'm dating Cardinal Cooke!

CUT TO:
INTERIOR. THE CARLYLE CLUB—NIGHT.

Bobby Short is playing "I'm In Love Again" on the piano, accompanied by a bass player. An Art Deco mural fills the wall behind him . . .

BOBBY SHORT *(Singing)* "Why am I / Just as reckless as a child? / Why am I / Like a racehorse running wild? / Why am I / In a state of ecstasy? / The reason is 'cause something's / Happened to me / I'm in love again / And the spring is comin' . . ."

. . . as the camera leaves the musicians and moves to the conservatively dressed audience. A far cry from the rock club atmosphere, the Carlyle is quiet except for Bobby Short's singing. The audience at their tables watch him, some with smiles of pleasure. A man has his arm around a woman. Jewels sparkle in another woman's hair. The men wear suits.

Mickey and Holly sit at one of the tables; a candle burns in its holder on the tabletop. Holly takes a cigarette from her purse as she holds her hand to her nose, sniffing. Mickey keeps shooting glances at Holly; she can't sit still. Bobby Short continues to sing . . .

BOBBY SHORT *(Singing)* "I'm in love again / Hear my heart strings strummin' / I'm in love again / And the hymn they're hummin' / Is those cuddle-up / huddle-up blues / I'm in love again / And I can't rise above it . . ."

. . . as Holly lights her cigarette, dropping her matchbook on the floor. She bends down to pick it up, then starts to fidget in her chair. She gulps her wine; she sniffs. Mickey tries to watch the offscreen Bobby Short; he crosses his arms across his chest.

The film cuts back briefly to Bobby Short playing the piano . . .

BOBBY SHORT *(Singing, continuing)* "I'm in love again / And I love, love, love it."

. . . then abruptly cuts to:

EXTERIOR. THE CARLYLE HOTEL—NIGHT.

A taxi pulls away from the curb as Mickey and Holly walk out of the hotel through its revolving doors. Holly stays under the awning;

HANNAH AND HER SISTERS

Mickey walks to the curb and looks angrily back at her. People pass by as Mickey walks back and forth from the curb to Holly, growing angrier and angrier.

HOLLY   Thanks for a swell time.

MICKEY *(Gesturing)*   Well, if you didn't like it, you didn't like it, but you didn't have to talk while the guy was singing.

HOLLY   I was so bored!

MICKEY *(Gesturing)*   Yeah, that's tough! You don't deserve Cole Porter. You should stay with those groups that look like they're gonna stab their mother!

HOLLY   At least I'm open to new concepts!

MICKEY   And you don't have to snort cocaine at the table all the time! What do you, what do you do? Carry a kilo around in your purse?

HOLLY *(Gesturing)*   This crowd wouldn't know the difference! They're embalmed!

MICKEY   Jesus . . . *(Waving his arm and whistling for a taxi)* I'm glad Hannah got us together. You know, she's got a great instinct for people. Really.
A taxi pulls up to the curb. Mickey and Holly walk up to its rear door.

HOLLY   Oh, look, I'm sorry it didn't work out.

MICKEY *(Overlapping)*   Yeah. Me, too.

HOLLY *(Overlapping)*   You know, it's probably my fault. I've been a little depressed lately.

MICKEY *(Overlapping)*   Right. Yeah. I had a . . .

HOLLY *(Overlapping)*   God!

MICKEY *(Continuing)* . . . I had a great time tonight, really. It was like the Nuremberg Trials.
He holds the door open for Holly. She gets in.

HOLLY *(Angrily)* Oh, I'll see myself home!
Holly slams the door. Mickey starts to walk along the sidewalk as the taxi drives off; he passes the hotel and several evening-lit store windows. "I'm In Love Again" begins to play in the background as Mickey's voice is heard.

MICKEY'S VOICE-OVER Yeah, it was quite an evening. Holly with her cocaine . . . *(Chuckling)* She should have been wearing a gold shovel around her neck. Tch, she was polymorphously insensitive, I think. *(Smacking his lips)* Too bad, too . . . 'cause, you know, I always had a little crush on her.
Both a bus and a taxi drive down the street, blocking Mickey from view. The music stops and the film cuts to:

*A big-band rendition of "You Made Me Love You" begins as the film
cuts to a hotel room. Elliot and Lee can be seen dancing cheek to cheek
in the reflection of a mirror over a dresser. A TV sits in the corner. A
lamp is on one side of the dresser; on the other side is a bucket with
champagne. Two half-full glasses sit nearby. Elliot and Lee dance into
view. Without missing a beat, Elliot picks up one of the glasses of
champagne and hands it to Lee. She sips. Elliot sips, then puts it back
down on the dresser. They embrace tightly, continuing to dance.*

CUT TO:
INTERIOR. HANNAH'S DINING ROOM—NIGHT.

*Elliot, Hannah, and the twins sit at the dining room table. A Christ-
mas tree stands in the corner of the room, next to a table holding a
lamp; a picture hangs on the wall. The family has just finished eating;
the table is cluttered with the remains of dinner, including a quart of
milk, some chocolate syrup, and a bottle of ketchup. Hannah's two
adopted children stand by her chair; she is showing them how a small
camera works. The children watch her, fascinated, muttering among
themselves. Elliot looks listless. He stares blankly at the table.*

HANNAH *(To her adopted children, holding the camera)* Oh, you just
have to read the instructions. I mean, you just set one of these
things and you can take, you can take pictures underwater.

CHILD #1 *(Overlapping)* Can I try it?

HANNAH *(Handing him the camera)* Sure! Yeah. When we get to
the country, we'll try it in the lake.
*The child takes the camera from Hannah, as well as picking up a
second identical one from the table.*

CHILD #1 Okay.

HANNAH *(Resting her chin in her hands)* Okay?

CHILD #2 *(Overlapping)* Can I go?

CHILD #1 *(Overlapping)*   Yeah.

HANNAH *(Nodding)*   Yeah! Okay.
> *The adopted children leave, the twins going off with them. When they're gone, Hannah takes a sip of her coffee and looks at Elliot. She puts down her cup, still watching him.*

HANNAH *(After a beat)*   Are you in a bad mood?

ELLIOT *(Shaking his head slightly)*   I don't know. Um . . . I'm just antsy.
> *The camera moves in on their faces as they continue to speak. Family photos line the mantel behind Hannah's head.*

HANNAH *(Intensely)*   Yes. I know. The last few weeks, you haven't been yourself. And tonight at, tonight at dinner, you, you were kind of curt with me.

ELLIOT *(Looking down at his hands)*   Was I?

HANNAH   Yes, you were. A-and when I, when I brought up the idea of having a baby, you just, you jumped down my throat.

ELLIOT *(Shaking his head)*   Well, I-I don't think it's a very good idea.

HANNAH   Why not?

ELLIOT *(Edgily)*   Because it's the last thing in the world we need right now.

HANNAH   Why do you say that? Is there something wrong?

ELLIOT   I don't know.

HANNAH   Well, tell me. Should I be worried?

ELLIOT   But, you got four children!

HANNAH   I want one with you.

ELLIOT   Well . . . I-I think we should wait till things settle.

HANNAH   But what do, what do you— *(Stuttering)* what's that mean? W-w-we've been, we've been married four years. How settled can things get?

ELLIOT *(Gesturing)*   You know, y-you have some very set plans on how your life should be structured. A-a house, uh, kids, certain schools, a h—, a home in Connecticut. I-it's all very . . . preconceived.

HANNAH *(Shaking her head)*   Yeah, but I . . . uh— I thought you needed that. When-when-when we met, you said your life was chaos.

ELLIOT   I-I-I know, but there's got to be some give and take.
Hannah sighs. Elliot angrily throws his napkin on the table. He stands up and begins to pace behind Hannah.

ELLIOT   Oh, let's not— I, I don't know what the hell I'm talking about.

HANNAH *(Reacting)*   Are you angry with me?

ELLIOT   No!

HANNAH   Do you feel, um . . . are you disenchanted with our marriage?

ELLIOT *(Pointing at Hannah)*   I didn't say that.

HANNAH   Are you in love with someone else?

ELLIOT *(Angrily)*   My God! Wha-what is this? The Gestapo? No.
He sits down again, in a chair next to Hannah; the ketchup bottle sits in front of him.

HANNAH *(Turning to look at him)*   Well, what? What, wh-what are you not telling me?

ELLIOT *(Gesturing and pointing)*   What kind of interrogation . . . Su-supposing I said yes? I-I-I am disenchanted. I am in love with someone else.

HANNAH   Are you?

ELLIOT *(Staring at Hannah for a beat before answering her)*   No! *(Gesturing)* But you keep asking these, these awful questions. My God, it's-it's like you want me to say yes!

HANNAH *(Gesturing)*   What, you, of c— What are you talking about? Of course not. I'd be destroyed!
The camera moves in on Elliot's anguished face. He talks over the screen.

ELLIOT'S VOICE-OVER   For Chrissakes, stop torturing her. Tell her you want out and get it over with. You're in love with her sister. You didn't do it on purpose. Be honest. It's always the best way.
He looks down. Hannah leans over and tenderly puts her hand on his shoulder.

HANNAH *(Softly)*   Look, can I help you? If you're suffering over something, will you share it with me?
She touches his hand; Elliot embraces her.

ELLIOT   Hannah, you know how much I love you. *(Kissing her on the forehead)* I ought to have my head examined. I don't deserve you.
Elliot kisses Hannah again; they embrace tightly. She touches his hair.

CUT TO:

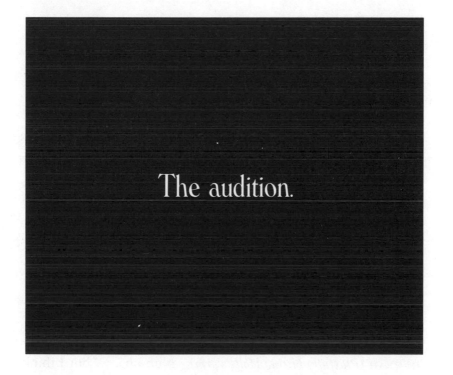

The audition.

There is no music.

CUT TO:
INTERIOR. SOHO CLOTHING BOUTIQUE—DAY.

The screen shows a metal staircase next to a large white column. Holly's voice can be heard as she and Hannah make their way up the stairs, moving into view. A man carrying a shopping bag walks down the steps; he passes them. Hannah and Holly talk as they climb.

HOLLY *(Offscreen)*   You know, I just want to look so good, but I don't want to seem, you know, like I'm overdressed. *(Onscreen, walking up the stairs behind Hannah)* You know what I'm saying?

HANNAH *(Overlapping, turning to look at Holly)*   Oh, no, not at all.

HOLLY *(Holding up a dress she's carrying on her arm)*   Well, how about this?

HANNAH *(Looking at the dress)*   Well, I, I really like that. I think that's a pretty color on you.

HOLLY *(Overlapping)*   Oh, yeah. *(Laughing)*
Hannah and Holly reach the top of the stairs. They walk onto a cavernous, high-tech floor. Empty bleachers line one wall; the rest of the floor is filled with racks of clothes and empty space.

HOLLY *(Continuing, smiling)*   Did you ever think you'd be helping me buy something to wear to the opera? *(Chuckling)*

HANNAH *(Playfully hitting Holly's arm)*   Nuh-uh . . . but I think it's great. I can't wait to meet him.
Holly follows Hannah to a rack of blouses.

HOLLY   He's married . . .

HANNAH *(Interrupting, looking through the rack)*   Oh-oh.

HOLLY *(Overlapping)* . . . and his wife's, uh, in and out of insti-
tutions. She's schizophrenic.
*Holly continues to talk as she follows Hannah across the floor to a rack
of dresses. Hannah's on one side, flipping through the hangers. Holly,
on the other side of the same rack, talks to her sister, not looking at
the clothes.*

HOLLY Sometimes she's terrific . . .

HANNAH *(Overlapping)* Oooo.

HOLLY . . . and then she just breaks down. *(Gesturing)* And he
has this sweet daughter . . . and when she goes to college next
year, he's going to split permanently. I mean . . .

HANNAH *(Overlapping, looking up at Holly)* Oh?

HANNAH . . . he's really paid his dues, but . . . then she
helped put him through architecture school, you know,
so . . .
*Hannah takes a jacket on a hanger off the rack and looks at it. She
holds it to her.*

HANNAH *(Interrupting, glancing at her sister for a moment with
amazement)* You found all this, all this out on one date?

HOLLY *(Chuckling and nodding)* Well, I think he was dying to
open up. It's so sad. *(Finally looking back and forth along the rack)*
Now . . . what should I wear to my audition?
*Hannah turns to Holly with surprise. She puts the jacket back on the
rack and stares at her; she inhales.*

HOLLY *(Explaining)* I've got a singing audition for a Broadway
musical. *(Chuckling)* Of course, I'll never get it.

HANNAH Singing?

HOLLY *(Chuckling)* Yeah, can you believe it?

HANNAH *(Walking around the rack to Holly, still surprised)* Really?

HOLLY *(Vulnerably)* Well, I mean, why not? You know, wh-what have I got to lose? Uh . . .

HANNAH *(Overlapping, shaking her head)* Well, no . . . I-I know, I just, uh . . . No, I-I, eh, you know, I, I didn't, I didn't know you sang.
Hannah begins to look at the rack of clothes on Holly's side, while her sister stares at her, frowning.

HOLLY *(Defensively)* Well, you think everybody in m-musicals sings so well?

HANNAH *(Gesturing, shaking her head)* No! No, I, eh, it's just that they sing.
Holly is silent for a moment. Hannah takes a blouse off the rack and looks at it.

HOLLY Well . . . you know, uh . . . I sing a little, I mean . . . *(Chuckling self-consciously)*

HANNAH *(Realizing she's hurt Holly, reacting)* Ohh!

HOLLY *(Overlapping, shaking her head)* You know.

HANNAH *(Hanging the blouse back on the rack)* I know, no— *(Chuckling)* I know.

HOLLY *(Overlapping, still chuckling self-consciously, gesturing)* I mean, y-you know, don't say it that way, you know, because my confidence is not my strong point, I—

HANNAH *(Interrupting, touching her sister's shoulder)* No, I'm sorry. No, I didn't mean that. No, I didn't mean that.
The two sisters walk away from the rack, Hannah slightly in the lead. Behind them are some more racks of clothing and a large window with closed venetian blinds.

HOLLY *(Gesturing)*   Uh, you know, I think I can fake my way through a song.

HANNAH *(Nodding as she looks around the store, pulling up her shoulder bag strap)*   Uh-huh.

HOLLY   Easily.
Holly pauses, looking at her sister. They continue to walk.

HOLLY *(Looking at Hannah)*   W-why? You don't think it's realistic?

HANNAH *(Putting her hand on Holly's shoulder)*   No, I didn't, I, that's, no. No, I-I-I, no, I-I just . . . *(Gesturing)* hate to see you put yourself in a position where, where you get hurt, you know. You know, you know how you take . . .

HOLLY *(Overlapping, nodding)*   Yeah.
They walk over to a table laid out with colorful scarves and decorated with hurricane lamps bordering its edges.

HANNAH *(Continuing, looking at some clothes hanging beneath the table)* . . . every, eh, single rejection as-as-as a . . . a confirmation that you have no talent, or something?

HOLLY *(Overlapping, nodding)*   Yeah. Well, maybe I'll get it. *(Chuckling and gesturing)*

HANNAH *(Overlapping, looking at the clothes)*   I hope.
Holly looks at her sister for a beat.

HOLLY *(Sighing)*   Boy, you really know how to cut me down.

HANNAH *(Looking at Holly, reacting)*   What? You don't, don't be so sensitive. Can't I say anything?

HOLLY *(Gesturing)*   Tch, well, I sing! *(Suddenly shouting)* For Chrissake, Hannah, you heard me sing!

A female customer, who'd come over to the table, browsing through the rack of clothes near Hannah, looks up, reacting. She walks away.

HANNAH *(Overlapping, reacting to her sister's outburst)* Okay! *(Looking at her sister)* Okay. I— What happened? You know, we were having a really nice time, a-and suddenly, everything went to bad feeling.
She walks past Holly and briefly looks at a different rack of clothes beneath the table.

HOLLY *(Shaking her head)* Nobody but you can do that to me. I don't know why.

HANNAH *(Gesturing)* Look, everything's going your way.
She walks offscreen to a nearby rack; the camera remains focused on Holly.

HOLLY You're right. *(Pausing)* I'm happy. *(Shrugging, looking at the offscreen Hannah)* Why must I let my insecurities spoil everything?
Holly chuckles and begins to look through the scarves on the table.

CUT TO:
INTERIOR. THEATER—DAY.

A group of theater executives, including the producer, the director, and two assistants, sit in a cluster in the empty audience, talking; they look up at the offscreen Holly, who is auditioning on the stage. She is singing "I'm Old-Fashioned," accompanied by a piano.

HOLLY *(Offscreen, singing softly)* "This year's fancies / Are passing fancies . . ."
The film moves from the audience to the stage where Holly, her hands clasped in front of her, continues to sing her song. A large group of other hopefuls are seen in the background behind her.

HOLLY *(Continuing her singing, barely moving her body)* "But sighing sighs / Holding hands / This my heart / Understands /

I'm old-fashioned / And I don't mind it / It's how I want to be / As long as you agree / To stay old-fashioned with me."
The camera moves from Holly back to the executives in the audience. As it passes the empty audience seats, they are heard offscreen.

PRODUCER *(Offscreen)*   Thank you.

DIRECTOR *(Offscreen)*   Thank you.

PRODUCER *(Offscreen)*   It was very nice.

ASSISTANT #1 *(Offscreen, overlapping)*   Terrific.
The camera has reached the executives in the audience. They are now chattering among themselves, Holly forgotten.

STAGE MANAGER *(Offscreen, overlapping the executives' chatter)* April Knox?
The film cuts back to the stage, where April, handing the audition pianist some sheet music, prepares herself to sing "The Way You Look Tonight." The stage is very black, stark, except for April and the pianist.

APRIL *(Singing)*   "Someday / When I'm awfully low / When the world is cold / I will get a glow / Just thinking of you / And the way you look / Tonight . . ."

CUT TO:
EXTERIOR. A STREET OUTSIDE THE THEATER—DAY.

A theater marquee can be seen on the busy street as Holly and April walk down the street towards the camera, moving closer and closer as they talk. Workmen and various street noises can be heard indistinctly in the background.

HOLLY   I'm telling you, you sounded great. You, uh, you may be surprised.

APRIL *(Sighing)*   Oh, I'm just glad we have a catering job this week. I'm real low on money.

HOLLY   Yeah, we have Mr. Morris Levine's eightieth birthday party on Riverside Drive . . . or Riverside Memorial Chapel, depending on his health.

APRIL   Oh, uh, listen, David called me up.

HOLLY *(Reacting)*   What?

APRIL *(Gesturing)*   Uh, David called me last night, and he wants to take me to the opera. *(Chuckling)* I didn't know what to say.

HOLLY *(Reacting)*   You're joking.

APRIL   No, he called late last night.

HOLLY *(Sadly)*   I, uh, I'm very surprised.

APRIL *(Chuckling, gesturing)*   He wants to take me to see *Rigoletto*.

HOLLY *(Looking briefly at April)*   And you, you-you're going?

APRIL   Well, I-I-I didn't know what to say. First I said no, but then, he pressed it. He said, uh, he'd taken you once and he really wanted to invite me.

HOLLY *(Pausing)*   But I'm seeing him.

APRIL *(Gesturing)*   I know. I said that, but . . . *(Shrugging)* he said it was something he really felt like doing.

HOLLY *(Stopping and facing April)*   Gee, um . . . *(Looking off, sniffing)* I . . . I don't know what to say.

APRIL   Look, it's just an evening at the opera. Did I, I-I do wrong in accepting?
Holly looks away sadly; she shakes her head.

APRIL *(Continuing)*   Huh?

   CUT TO:

The big leap.

The film cuts to Father Flynn's rectory office. The Catholic priest looks out a simple stained-glass window, then turns to an offscreen Mickey.

FATHER FLYNN *(Gesturing)* Now why do you think that you would like to convert to Catholicism?
The camera moves back to reveal Mickey, his back to the camera, sitting in front of Father Flynn's desk. A lamp is lit in the background; the Father's desk is neat. The room is comfortably decorated in wood and leather.

MICKEY Well, uh, because, y-you know, I gotta have something to believe in, otherwise life is just meaningless.

FATHER FLYNN *(Pacing behind his desk and gesturing)* I understand. But why did you make the decision to choose the Catholic faith?

The movie cuts to Mickey's face. He's very neat in a tie, sweater, and sports jacket.

MICKEY *(Gesturing)*   Tch. Well, y-you know . . . first of all, because it's a very beautiful religion. It's very well structured. Now I'm talking now, incidentally, about the-the, uh, against-school-prayer, pro-abortion, anti-nuclear wing.

FATHER FLYNN *(Offscreen)*   So at the moment you don't believe in God.
The camera cuts back to Father Flynn, who walks over to a leather armchair next to a table set for tea. He begins to pour the tea into china cups.

MICKEY *(Offscreen)*   No. A-a-and I-I want to. You know, I'm-I'm willing to do anything. I'll, you know, I'll dye Easter eggs if it works. *(Walking over to Father Flynn and sitting down in an adjacent chair)* I-I need some evidence. I gotta have some proof. Uh, you know, i-i-if I can't believe in God *(Gesturing, his raincoat in his lap)* then I don't think life is worth living.

FATHER FLYNN *(Stopping his tea pouring)*   It means making a very big leap.
Father Flynn clasps his hands in his lap.

MICKEY *(Nodding, fiddling with his raincoat)*   Yes, well, can-can you help me?
The film abruptly cuts to the long hallway in Mickey's parents' apartment. In the foreground, a section of the living room can be seen, with a bureau holding a lamp and a framed photo. The hallway itself is crowded with pictures and a wall shelf. At the other end of the hallway, in the background, is another bureau, with candlesticks on top and a framed picture on the wall above. Mickey's mother stands in the front of this bureau at the hallway's end, screaming at the top of her lungs, holding her heart dramatically.

MOTHER *(Crying)*   Why? Oh, my God!

She sobs hysterically, staggering offscreen to the bathroom; she shuts the door. Mickey walks into view, in the living room, looking after his shocked mother, who continues to cry over the scene.

MICKEY *(Overlapping and gesturing)*   I don't understand. *(Turning to his offscreen father)* I thought that you would be happy.

FATHER *(Offscreen)*   How can we be happy?
His father walks into view, carrying a teacup and a candy dish. He strides past Mickey towards the kitchen.

MICKEY *(Following his father)*   Well, because I never thought of God in my life. Now I'm giving it serious thought.

FATHER *(Offscreen, in the kitchen)*   But Catholicism? Why not your own people?

MICKEY *(Gesturing at the kitchen door to his offscreen father)*   Because I got off to a wrong foot with my own thing, you know. B-b-b-but I need a dramatic change in my life.

FATHER *(Offscreen)*   You're gonna believe in Jesus Christ?

MICKEY *(Gesturing)*   I know it sounds funny, but I'm gonna try.

FATHER *(Offscreen)*   But why? We raised you as a Jew.

MICKEY *(Shrugging)*   So, just 'cause I was born that way . . . You know, I'm old enough to make a mature decision.
Mickey's father walks into view; he stands by the stove near the kitchen doorway, picking up a dirty glass and some bowls to clean.

FATHER   But why Jesus Christ? Why, for instance, shouldn't you become a Buddhist?
Holding the dirty dishes in his hand, Mickey's father looks at his son.

MICKEY *(Gesturing)*   A Bud—? That's totally alien to me. Look, you're getting on in years, right? Aren't you afraid of dying?
Mickey's father walks offscreen again, to the kitchen sink.

FATHER *(Offscreen)*   Why should I be afraid?

MICKEY *(Loudly gesturing)*   Oh! 'Cause you won't exist!

FATHER *(Offscreen)*   So?

MICKEY *(Gesturing)*   That thought doesn't terrify you?
Mickey's father walks out of the kitchen, past his son, to the living room.

FATHER *(Waving his arm)*   Who thinks about such nonsense? Now I'm alive. When I'm dead, I'll be dead.

MICKEY *(Following his father, gesturing)*   I don't understand. Aren't you frightened?

FATHER *(Offscreen)*   Of what? I'll be unconscious.

MICKEY *(Turning and walking down the hallway)*   Yeah, I know. But never to exist again!

FATHER *(Offscreen)*   How do you know?

MICKEY   Well, it certainly doesn't look promising.
Mickey stops at the bathroom door at the other end of the hallway. He starts to pound it.

FATHER *(Offscreen)*   Who knows what'll be?
Mickey's father comes back on screen; he's carrying a plate of hors d'oeuvres and an empty glass towards the kitchen. He stops and looks down the hall at Mickey, who's now struggling to open the bathroom door.

FATHER *(Gesturing with his hands full)*   I'll either be unconscious or I won't. If not, I'll deal with it then. I'm not gonna worry now about what's gonna be when I'm unconscious.

MICKEY *(Pounding on the door)*   Mom, come out!

MOTHER *(Offscreen in the bathroom)*   Of course there's a God, you idiot! You don't believe in God?

MICKEY *(Sighing)*   But if there's a God, then wh-why is there so much evil in the world? *(Shrugging)* Wha— Just on a simplistic level. Why-why were there Nazis?

MOTHER *(Offscreen in the bathroom)*   Tell him, Max.
Mickey, reacting, hits his forehead.

FATHER *(Offscreen)*   How the hell do I know why there were Nazis? I don't know how the can opener works.
Mickey starts pounding the door again as the movie cuts to:

A beautiful snow-covered church downtown, complete with courtyard and wrought-iron fence. A pedestrian walks by with an umbrella. A church choir sings a soaring hymn over the scene.

The music continues as the film moves inside, where the choir is seen singing behind an altar glowing warm gold. A fairly large congregation sits in darkened pews as the film cuts to the back, where Mickey, his arms crossed, stands underneath some stained-glass windows, watching and listening to the inspiring music.

The choir continues to sing as the movie cuts to Father Flynn in his office. He picks up some large, heavy books from a shelf near his window and he walks over to Mickey, who's standing near his desk, already holding several tomes. Father Flynn puts the books on top of Mickey's pile; Mickey, flipping through the top one, awkwardly carries his bundle to the door.

Next is seen a close-up of a painting of Jesus Christ on the cross, complete with crown of thorns and holy expression. His eyes, especially designed to blink as the lights hit them, open and close repeatedly. The hymn plays on, loudly, as the camera moves back, revealing Mickey, standing outside a barber shop window, looking at the Christ painting and shuffling from side to side to gets its eyes' 3-D effect. Smaller inspirational pictures border the bigger, blinking Christ. A barber pole with moving stripes stands nearby; passing traffic is reflected in the window.

Mickey turns from the window, shrugging, and starts to walk down the street, past a fruit and vegetable store with open-air-displayed flowers, past several briskly moving pedestrians.

With the hymn still playing, the screen goes black briefly. Mickey opens the door, the light from a hallway illuminating him. He's just entered his apartment. He closes the door and walks through his dark foyer; he carries a brown bag. He switches on the light, and walking past his spiral staircase, past several framed pictures on the wall, he makes his way to his living room coffee table. Mickey pulls a crucifix out of the bag; he looks at it, then puts it on the table near a pile of books and some objets d'art. He then takes out a copy of the New Testament, putting it on top of the crucifix. Then out comes a framed picture of a saint. It too gets put on the growing pile. But the bag is not yet empty. Next comes a large loaf of Wonder Bread and a large jar of Hellman's mayonnaise. Mickey sets them on top of the saint.

CUT TO:
EXTERIOR. NEW YORK STREET—DAY.

Lee is walking down the street, looking around her. The sidewalk is fairly crowded with people; the sounds of traffic are heard. She passes some office buildings, a store's large display window; she stops when she sees Hannah. Her sister is waiting outside the Art Deco façade of a restaurant; she's looking in the opposite direction. Lee taps Hannah on the shoulder; Hannah, surprised, turns and gasps.

LEE *(Overlapping Hannah's gasp)*   Hi.
The sisters laugh and embrace each other.

HANNAH   Hi. Where's Holly?

LEE *(Overlapping)* Hi. She's auditioning for a television commercial. She said she's gonna be a little late.

HANNAH *(Sighing)* Oh, yeah? How's she doing?
She turns and walks towards the restaurant entrance.

LEE *(Following Hannah through the restaurant's doors)* Oh, God, you know Holly. When she's depressed, she's manic. I think it was a good idea that we invited her to lunch.
They disappear inside. The camera follows them, cutting to the restaurant's interior at the same time the sisters walk in. It's a chic, trendy place, with an Art Deco design and high ceilings. A waiter in uniform stands near its glass and metal doors, holding a tray to his chest; a few people sit at the bar; a large plant in a vase sits in the foreground. The sisters walk toward the coatcheck area, deep in conversation.

HANNAH *(Pulling off her scarf, still on the subject of Holly)* I hope you tell her it was your idea . . .

LEE Why?

HANNAH *(Overlapping)* . . . 'cause every time I try to be helpful, you know, sh-she gets so defensive.

LEE *(Unbuttoning her coat)* Oh, Hannah, she's-she's just embarrassed in front of you, that's all.
Hannah walks offscreen, farther into the coatcheck room. She talks offscreen as Lee alone is seen, reacting and speaking as well. In the background, a waiter crosses over to the bar, then walks away.

HANNAH *(Offscreen)* So how are you?

LEE Oh, me, I'm okay.

HANNAH *(Offscreen)* Do you miss Frederick?

LEE No.

HANNAH *(Offscreen)*   I can't believe Elliot and I can't think of someone nice for you to go out with, you know—

LEE *(Interrupting, her voice slightly higher-pitched as she takes off her coat)*   How are you?

HANNAH *(Offscreen)*   I'm okay.

LEE *(Overlapping)*   You know, how's everything? You doing okay? How's Frederick? *(Laughing)* I mean, Elliot.

HANNAH *(Offscreen, overlapping)*   Y-yeah.
Hannah walks out of the coatcheck room without her coat; it's Lee's turn to disappear and check her things. Now only Hannah can be seen onscreen as the sisters talk. In the background, the waiter once again walks over to the bar.

HANNAH *(Continuing)*   Oh, he's fine. He's-he's, I guess he's fine. I don't know. *(Shaking her head, her arms crossed)* He's been kinda moody lately, the last few months.

LEE *(Offscreen, overlapping)*   Really?

HANNAH   Yeah. I-I don't know what's wrong with him. He's just . . . kind of distant and difficult.

LEE *(Offscreen)*   Oh . . .

HANNAH *(Overlapping, gesturing)*   I've been trying to talk to him about it. He says everything's fine, but I don't know. Automatically, you know, I leap to the worst conclusions.

LEE *(Offscreen)*   Like what?
As Hannah answers her sister, Holly can be seen entering the restaurant and walking over to the coatcheck area, an unlit cigarette in her mouth, her sunglasses still on her eyes.

HANNAH *(Gesturing)*   I mean, I don't know, he's seeing someone else or something, but . . .

LEE *(Walking back onscreen without her coat, reacting)* Oh, no! I mean, everyone thinks things like that.
Hannah mumbles indistinctly as Holly walks over to her sisters.

HANNAH *(Turning, to Holly)* Hey, hi!

HOLLY *(Overlapping)* Well, I just came from an audition . . .

LEE *(Overlapping, leaning against the coatcheck wall)* Hi.

HOLLY *(Continuing)* . . . which I did not get.

HANNAH *(Reacting)* Awwww . . .

HOLLY *(Overlapping, sighing)* So what's new?
She takes off her gloves and scarf, stuffing them in her bag.

HANNAH *(Helping Holly with her coat)* Boy—

HOLLY *(Interrupting)* They said I was too offbeat looking, whatever the hell that means.

HANNAH Oh, what do they know?
Holly gives her coat to the coatcheck person.

HOLLY *(To the checker)* Thanks. *(Turning to her sisters)* But guess who was there auditioning?

LEE April?
The hostess appears, peeking around the corner of the coatcheck area. She signals for the three sisters to follow her.

HANNAH *(Reacting to Holly's news)* Oh, gosh.

HOLLY You got it.
Holly takes off her sunglasses; her cigarette still dangles from her mouth. Hannah murmurs her sympathy as the trio follows the hostess into the dining room.

HOLLY *(Gesturing)* I was very polite. I maintained my poise. *(Taking out a match for her cigarette)* I said hello.

The sisters walk to their seats, at a round table in the middle of the room; the hostess puts down their menus.

LEE   Hmm. I never trusted April, you know. She has eyes in the back of her head.
They sit down. The hostess leaves. Other diners are seen in the background; a waiter is taking the order of a couple sitting on a banquette; other waiters clear off a table. Diners walk in and out. A low murmur of conversation, as well as the faint clatter of dishes, is heard. The camera moves closer to the three sisters, circling the table as Holly speaks.

HOLLY   Yeah, well, she and an architect are now a very definite item, which I still cannot believe.

LEE *(Overlapping)*   Hmm.

HANNAH   Oh, God . . .

HOLLY *(Nodding her head, holding her cigarette)*   Yeah, although it's put an end to the Stanislavski Catering Company. Which is why I have to speak to you. And . . . *(Gesturing to Hannah)* you're gonna get impatient, but . . . I have to borrow some more money. *(Putting her cigarette in her mouth and picking up the matches)*

HANNAH *(Shaking her head)*   Well, that . . . th-that's fine.

HOLLY *(Gesturing, her cigarette in one hand, her matches in the other)*   But what I decided to do is some writing. Yeah, I think I've had it with acting. You know, these meaningless auditions at cattle calls. And I can't handle another rejection. *(Emotionally)* Now let's face it here. I gotta, you know, latch on to something in my life. You know—something with a future. I'm not sixteen anymore. *(Lighting her cigarette)* It's just . . . crazy! But . . . *(Puffing her cigarette)* I've got . . . an idea for a story. More than one. And I just need a few months, you know, or, uh, a year even.

As the camera slowly circles the table, Hannah is seen listening to Holly, her hand on her mouth.

HOLLY   I've picked up a lot about dramatic structure from doing my scenes in acting class.

Lee, her hand on her mouth, glances briefly at Hannah. As Hannah replies to Holly, the camera focuses on Lee's face. She bites her nails; she looks down, involved in her own thoughts.

HANNAH *(Offscreen)*   Well, that-that's good. It just, uh . . . it just seems to me that-that six months or a year, if-if you spent it more productively . . .

HOLLY *(Offscreen, the camera still focused on Lee)*   Well-well, like what?

Lee looks up, her hand still on her mouth, watching Hannah, as the camera slowly moves off her to show Hannah.

HANNAH   Well, I don't know. We'd uh, uh, um . . . Didn't Mom mention there was something . . . something at the Museum of Broadcasting?

HOLLY *(Offscreen)*   Yeah, that's clerical.

HANNAH   No. She, didn't she say it was, um . . . she said it was in the publicity department. That-that can lead to other things.

The camera is back on Lee. She looks around tensely, barely listening to the conversation. She fidgets. An empty table sits in the background.

HOLLY *(Offscreen)*   Boy, I knew you'd be discouraging.

HANNAH *(Offscreen)*   I'm not! I'm not! I'm trying to be helpful. A person doesn't just say one day, "Okay, now-now I'm finished as an actress. Now I'm a writer." I mean—

HOLLY *(Offscreen, interrupting)*   Yeah, you mean not at my age.

LEE *(Shaking her head, unable to take much more)*   Oh, please! We all came to have lunch, didn't we?

HOLLY *(Reacting, now in view)*   Yeah, okay, right. Forget it. *(Puffing on her cigarette)* What's to eat?
Holly abruptly picks up her menu.

LEE *(Trying to alleviate the tension)*   Boy . . . Holly . . . Holly.

HOLLY *(Overlapping)*   I just want a salad. *(To Hannah)* You really think I'm a loser, don't you?

HANNAH *(Offscreen)*   What do—? You're being ridiculous.

LEE *(Overlapping, reacting)*   You are, Holly. Stop it.

HOLLY *(To Hannah)*   You treat me like a loser.

HANNAH *(Offscreen)*   How?

HOLLY   You never have any faith in my plans. You always undercut my enthusiasm.
She puffs intensely on her cigarette as the camera slowly circles to Hannah's face. She is equally intense, looking at both sisters as she speaks.

HANNAH   Not so! No. I think I've been very supportive. I've . . . I try to give you honest, constructive advice.

HOLLY *(Offscreen)*   Hmm!

HANNAH *(Overlapping)*   I'm-I'm always happy to help you financially. I think I've gone out of my way to-to introduce you to interesting single men. There's nothing I would—

HOLLY *(Offscreen, interrupting)*   Uh, losers! All losers!

HANNAH   You're too demanding.

HOLLY *(Offscreen)* You know, I could always tell what you thought of me by the type of men you fixed me up with!
The camera, slowly circling the table, is back on Lee's face. While her sisters argue emotionally on her right and left, she is looking down, biting her lip. She is outwardly still, but her face is registering her seething emotions.

HANNAH *(Offscreen)* You're crazy! That's not true.

HOLLY *(Offscreen)* Hey, Hannah, I know I'm mediocre.

LEE *(Interrupting angrily, looking as if she's about to cry)* Oh, will you stop attacking Hannah?!

HANNAH *(Offscreen, overlapping)* Oh, now— *(Stuttering)*

LEE *(Interrupting, shaking her head)* She's going through a really rough time right now.

HOLLY *(Offscreen)* Why are *you* so upset?

LEE *(Sobbing and gesturing)* You know, you've been picking on her ever since she came in here. Now just leave her alone for a while! I'm just suffocating. *(Sniffing back her tears)*

HOLLY *(Leaning over to Lee, puzzled, reacting to her sister's tears)* What's the matter with you, Lee? Why are you so sensitive all of a sudden?

HANNAH *(Offscreen)* Look. *(Onscreen, as the camera circles around the table)* Listen. Listen. *(Tapping Holly on her shoulder and gesturing)* You want to write? Write.

HOLLY *(Offscreen, overlapping to Lee)* What's the matter?

HANNAH *(Flinging her hands)* Write! Let's just not talk about it anymore.

HOLLY *(Offscreen)* Good.

HANNAH *(Shaking her head)* Take . . . take a year. Take six months. Whatever you want. Who knows? Maybe you'll, maybe you'll be sitting with a good play.
She opens her menu, then turns to Lee, reacting suddenly to her sister, who is rubbing her forehead, looking terribly upset.

HANNAH *(To Lee)* What's the matter? What's the matter with you? *(Offscreen again as the camera circles back to Lee)* You look pale. You okay?

LEE *(Overlapping, nodding and stuttering)* I'm-I'm okay. Yeah, I-I-I, you know, I . . . I'm just, um, I got dizzy all of a sudden. I'm-I'm . . . I have a headache.

HANNAH *(Offscreen, overlapping)* Yeah?

LEE *(Still rubbing her forehead, looking down at the menu)* I think we need to eat.

CUT TO:

Summer in New York.

A piano plays "Bewitched" in the background as the film cuts to a large tree, covered with bright white blossoms. The camera moves down the tree to reveal a well-kept, red-brick brownstone on a pleasant, sunny New York City street. A man wearing a summer suit walks by as the film moves inside the building, to Elliot's analyst's office. The psychotherapist sits in a comfortable armchair next to a curtained window. In front of the window sits a table covered with artifacts and a large lamp. The analyst's fingers are touching, his arms resting on the chair, as he listens to the offscreen Elliot.

ELLIOT *(Offscreen)*   I-I can't seem to take action. I'm-I'm like, uh, Hamlet unable to kill his uncle.
The music stops as the camera moves across the room to reveal Elliot, sitting in a wooden chair. He holds a long, thin cigarette; he wears a gold Rolex watch. His face is not yet seen.

ELLIOT *(Face offscreen)*   I want Lee, but I can't harm Hannah. And in no other area am I a procrastinator.
Elliot raises his cigarette to take a drag. The camera follows the cigarette up to his face. Elliot looks thoughtful as the movie cuts to:

EXTERIOR. COLUMBIA UNIVERSITY CAMPUS—DAY.

Lee, wearing jeans and carrying an armful of books, is running up a broad set of steps in the sunlight, greeting other students as she passes. Elliot continues to talk over the scene . . .

ELLIOT'S VOICE-OVER   Meanwhile . . . Lee has no direction. She's taking courses at Columbia . . . but just randomly.

. . . as Lee stops on a portico and turns to greet Doug, a professor, who is running over to her, calling her name. They mouth hello, smiling, and begin to walk off together.

ELLIOT'S VOICE-OVER   I try not to call her, but then she calls me and then . . . I call and . . . we try to resist meeting, but . . . once in a while we meet. Sometimes we argue because I can't

break up my marriage. Sometimes we wind up making love and . . . we both feel terrible.
The film cuts back to Elliot in his analyst's office.

ELLIOT   But it's my fault.
Elliot takes a last drag on his cigarette. The camera follows his hand as he crushes it out in a nearby ashtray.

ELLIOT *(Face offscreen)*   For all my education, accomplishments, and so-called wisdom . . . I can't fathom my own heart.

CUT TO:
EXTERIOR. CENTRAL PARK—DAY.

Hare Krishna music is heard over a sunlit view of the Manhattan skyline and the green trees of Central Park. The camera moves down to reveal a large group of Hare Krishnas dancing on the broad green lawn among other New Yorkers enjoying the day. The leader, holding some pamphlets, stands by a chain-link fence, a few feet away from his group, talking to someone on the other side. It's Mickey, as the camera soon shows, wearing a short-sleeved shirt, a paper tucked under his arm.

KRISHNA LEADER   What makes you interested in becoming a Hare Krishna?

MICKEY *(Gesturing, walking onscreen)*   Well, I'm not saying that I want to join or anything, but . . . but I know you guys believe in reincarnation, you know, so it interests me.

KRISHNA LEADER   Yeah, well, what's your religion?

MICKEY *(Gesturing)*   Well, I was born Jewish, you know, but, uh, but last winter I tried to become a Catholic and . . . it didn't work for me. I-I studied and I tried and I gave it everything, but, you know, Catholicism for me was die now, pay later, you know. And I just couldn't get with it. And I, and I wanted to, you know. I—

HANNAH AND HER SISTERS

KRISHNA LEADER *(Interrupting)* You're afraid of dying?

MICKEY *(Gesturing)* Well . . . yeah, naturally. Aren't you? I—
L-let me ask you, reincarnation, does that mean my soul
would pass to another human being, or would I come back as
a moose or an aardvark or something?

KRISHNA LEADER *(Handing some Krishna literature over the fence to
Mickey)* Take our literature . . .

MICKEY *(Nodding, taking the material)* Uh-huh.

KRISHNA LEADER . . . read it over, and think about it.

MICKEY *(Looking down at the material he's just received)* Well, okay.
Thank you very much.

KRISHNA LEADER You're welcome. Hare Krishna.
*Mickey walks off, the Hare Krishnas still dancing and singing on
the other side of the fence. He flips through the literature as he walks,
then looks straight ahead, pondering. His voice is heard over the
screen.*

MICKEY'S VOICE-OVER Who are you kidding? You're gonna be a
Krishna? You're gonna shave your head and put on robes and
dance around at airports? You'll look like Jerry Lewis. Oh,
God, I'm so depressed.
*Mickey puts his hand to his mouth as another title appears on a black
screen.*

Autumn chill.

Bach's Concerto for Harpsichord is heard as the film cuts to the water-front at dusk. A bench faces some wharf pilings; the water gently laps against them as Lee walks into view, the wind blowing her hair. She stands and faces the water and the distant skyline across the bay. The view is contemplative, beautiful in the dim light. Lee is alone; her hands are in her pockets. Lee, thinking, is heard over the scene; the harpsichord music plays in the background.

LEE'S VOICE-OVER   The nights are really getting cooler. Summer went so quickly. Soon it'll be fall. *(Walking to the bench and sitting down)* My literature professor really likes me. It was fun being out with him last night. *(Staring pensively at the water)* Funny. I feel like I'm betraying Elliot . . . but that's ridiculous. Why shouldn't I see Doug? Elliot's not free. *(Pausing)* Just go one step at a time. Let's see what the next few months bring.

The concerto stops and the movie cuts to Holly, leaning into an open phone booth near a subway entrance. She wears a football jacket, jeans, and sneakers; she holds a manuscript in her arms. It's a busy corner. People rush past Holly towards the subway; others are walking up the station steps. Holly smokes a cigarette as she talks on the phone to Hannah.

HOLLY *(Into the telephone)* Hannah? Hi. Listen, um, you'll be happy to know that your money has not gone completely to waste . . . No, I have an actual first rough draft of something I wrote . . . Yeah. Yeah. Yeah, well, I showed it to Lee, and she gave me some good pointers. And, um, listen, I'm pretty near where you live. I wonder if I could just drop it off . . . and, you know, when you have time, some time, read it, an- and we'll talk when I come over at Thanksgiving. Okay? All right. Okay. Oh, wait, wait. *(Turning her body, still on the phone)* Listen. Listen. I think Lee met an interesting guy at Columbia . . . Yeah. Yeah, well, he sounds really nice . . . *(Puffing on her cigarette)* Yeah. Okay. All right. Well, we'll talk at Thanksgiving. Bye-bye.
Holly hangs up the phone and takes a drag on her cigarette. She looks off in the distance, smiling, as the film cuts to:

INTERIOR. HANNAH'S APARTMENT—THANKSGIVING NIGHT.

It's Thanksgiving at Hannah's once again. Guests are crowded together in the living room, surrounding the piano, where Evan is sitting and flipping through some sheet music. Norma stands behind him, leaning against a book-laden wall. The guests are chattering, enjoying themselves; a lamp glows on the corner of the piano. A little boy sitting in a chair next to Evan is talking animatedly with a girl who is leaning over the arm of the sofa. An adult guest talks to the little boy; another guest takes a sip of wine from a glass she'd placed on the bookshelf behind her as Evan turns and addresses the group.

EVAN *(Gesturing)* Now, here . . . here's a song that Norma sang on that trip we made up to the show in Buffalo. And, oh, was she beautiful that night!
The guests laugh appreciatively. A woman comes over to Evan and hands him some wine.

NORMA Come on. *(Laughing and touching Evan's shoulder)*

EVAN *(Overlapping, to the woman)* Thank you, honey. *(Putting his drink down on the piano)* Oh, yes, you were, dear. Don't you remember that night? *(Gesturing and pushing back some sheet music that was starting to fall)* She was so beautiful . . . she was so beautiful that when men saw her walking along the streets, they'd drive their cars right up on the sidewalk.
He laughs; the guests laugh with him.

EVAN *(Looking back at Norma)* Isn't that right, honey, eh?

NORMA *(Tapping his shoulder)* A slight exaggeration.
The guests continue to laugh; they are charmed.

EVAN *(Overlapping Norma, laughing)* I know.

NORMA *(Gesturing)* But only slight.
Evan continues to laugh with everyone as he starts to play the piano. A nearby woman toasts him with her drink. The camera moves around the room as he plays, showing the various guests, chattering over the music. Some are in clusters, in private conversations; others listen and watch the offscreen Evan. A couple stands by the window; one man gets up from his chair and walks away. Some guests sip their drinks, smiling, as the camera moves back to the piano and the book-laden wall. Evan is playing the piano with exuberance. Norma, still standing behind him, has a poignant, wistful expression on her face. She mouths the words to the song Evan is playing, "It Could Happen to You." The woman next to her smiles, enjoying the music, as the camera continues its exploration, moving to a man standing in the doorway with a group of children. Mavis the maid walks by with a

tray of hors d'oeuvres. The man takes one, mouthing his thanks, as the camera travels past the open bookshelf, past two boys in suits who are drinking soda and munching, to reveal Lee. She is leaning against another doorway, a faraway look on her face as she listens to the music. Mavis passes in the hall beyond the doorway. Several people, deep in conversation, stand nearby as Elliot, holding a drink, walks up behind her.

ELLIOT *(Sipping his drink)*   You've been very cold to me tonight.

LEE *(Glancing back at Elliot, then turning away)*   No.

ELLIOT   Is something wrong?

LEE *(Turning)*   Oh, not here. *(Touching Elliot's arm)* There are too many people around.
Lee slips past Elliot and walks away. Elliot looks back at her briefly, then, sipping his drink, he turns and looks offscreen at the crowd in the living room.

CUT TO:
INTERIOR. HANNAH'S KITCHEN—NIGHT.

Holly is standing in the pantry, preparing some offscreen food. Near her is a restaurantlike swinging door with a glass porthole. In the foreground, the kitchen table is crowded with bowls and plates of food. An open cupboard separates Holly from the rest of the room.

HOLLY *(Looking offscreen)*   Hey, Hannah? You know, I think Lee is really serious about her new boyfriend. Yeah, eh, from what I understand he sounds really nice.
Hannah walks into view, headed for the refrigerator. She carries two tomatoes.

HOLLY   I'm so happy for her. I think she's in love.
Hannah opens the refrigerator, totally ignoring Holly.

HOLLY *(Reacting)*   Hey, what's the matter?

HANNAH *(Taking a bunch of celery out and slamming the refrigerator door)* I'm real upset about what you wrote.
Hannah walks over to the table, gathering up more food.

HOLLY My script?

HANNAH It's obviously based on Elliot and me.

HOLLY Oh, so loosely.

HANNAH *(Angrily)* No, not "Oh, so loosely"! Real specifically! Is that how you see us?

HOLLY *(Shrugging, walking out of the pantry area)* Well—

HANNAH *(Interrupting)* Can I, can I not accept gestures and feelings from people? Do I, do I put people off?
Holly walks over to the sink and washes her hands.

HOLLY *(Reacting)* Well, it's a made-up story.
She dries her hands as Hannah, her arms laden with vegetables, strides over to her sister.

HANNAH *(Yelling)* No, it's real exact! The-the situations, the dialogue, everything. It's-it's full of intimate details between Elliot and me! Which I don't, I don't see how you could even possibly know about. A conversation we once had about adoption?
Hannah storms out a nearby door as Holly turns away from the sink.

HOLLY *(Gesturing, the towel still in her hand, as she speaks to her offscreen sister)* Well, Lee mentioned that to me, so obviously you discussed it with her. You . . . *(Pacing around the table)* I just took the essence and I blew it up into drama.
Holly wipes her hand on the towel as Hannah reenters the kitchen, carrying even more vegetables.

HANNAH I don't see how Lee could know about these things. I don't! I don't tell her everything.

Hannah strides into the pantry area and flops the vegetables down on the counter. Holly puts the dishtowel down and absently straightens some things on the food-laden table.

HOLLY *(Reacting)*   Wow, I guess I hit a nerve.

HANNAH *(Turning to look at Holly)*   You make it sound like, you know, I have no needs or something. You think I'm too self-sufficient?

HOLLY *(Stopping her mindless straightening at the table, reacting)*   Now, Hannah, that's not what I meant, you know. *(Walking offscreen to the sink area)* Uh, yeah, everybody relies on you for so much. "You're so giving. It's not a criticism. We love you. We're grateful.

HANNAH *(Walking out of the pantry to the food-laden table)* You're grateful, but you resent me.

HOLLY *(Offscreen)*   Oh, wow! I don't want to have this conversation. I didn't do anything wrong.
Hannah angrily gathers up some spices from the table; Holly walks back onscreen holding a silver ice bucket. She stops at the corner of the table and faces Hannah.

HOLLY *(Onscreen)*   Y-you mentioned to me yourself that you and Elliot were having some problems.

HANNAH *(Gesturing)*   Yeah, we're having some problems, but problems that are *my* business . . . which I don't see how you could know about in such detail. How does Lee know about these things? How? They're private!
Hannah picks up a large bowl and carries it, as well as her armload of spices, into the pantry area.

HOLLY *(Turning to look at her sister as she walks past)*   Well, why don't you share them with us?

HANNAH *(With her back to the camera)*   I don't . . . I don't want to bother everyone.

HOLLY *(Facing her sister's back)*   That's the point. I'd like to be bothered.

HANNAH *(Turning to look at Holly)*   I don't see how you could know about these things unless Elliot's been talking to you.

HOLLY *(Shaking her head)*   No, he hasn't. If I offended you, I'm sorry.
Hannah, reacting, puts the spices down on the pantry counter. Holly turns away.

The film cuts to the dining room doorway. Guests can be seen mingling and talking and helping themselves at a buffet table in the living room. Lee and Elliot can be heard offscreen as the camera slowly moves from the doorway across the empty dining room to reveal them in the midst of an intense conversation. The piano, as well as soft chatter, is heard in the background.

LEE *(Offscreen)*   It's over, Elliot. I don't know how to make it any clearer. It's over. I can't see you anymore.

ELLIOT *(Offscreen, overlapping)*   Uh . . . *(Onscreen, gesturing)* I-I-I know. I deserve this.

LEE *(Touching her chest)*   Look, I'm just as much at fault.

ELLIOT *(Overlapping, gesturing)*   If-if-if you can believe I have such feelings for you!

LEE   I've got to be honest with you. I met someone else. I've met someone else. *(Turning and walking away from Elliot)* I . . . I told you I wasn't going to wait forever.
Lee goes over to an open door and closes it quickly.

ELLIOT *(Offscreen)*   But it hasn't been forever. *(Walking over to Lee at the just-closed door.)*

LEE *(Gesturing)* It's been nearly a year since our first time and you're still married to my sister, which . . . I now realize is fine because you're probably much more in love with her than you know.

ELLIOT *(Shaking his head)* Yeah, but we-we made so many plans.

LEE *(Overlapping, gesturing)* Yeah. Uh, well, sure we did. An-an-and in a way you led me on, because I truly believed you were unhappy with Hannah. Otherwise, I would never have let myself be drawn in. I was very weak. So were you. Now I've met someone else.
The door opens and Mavis appears, holding a set of candlesticks. She walks over to the dining room table, which is already decked out with a floral centerpiece, glassware, and china. She puts them down as Lee and Elliot stand awkwardly near the door, waiting for her to leave.

LEE *(To Mavis)* Dinner soon?

MAVIS About fifteen minutes.

LEE *(Nodding)* Uh-huh. Good.
Mavis leaves. Both Lee and Elliot quickly close the door behind her and immediately pick up where they'd left off.

ELLIOT And you're in love overnight?

LEE I care a great deal about him, yes.

ELLIOT *(Trying to put his arm around Lee)* Lee . . .

LEE *(Pulling back, flinging her hands)* Ah, it's over! Elliot, I mean it. It's over!
They look at each other, reacting, as the film cuts back to Hannah's kitchen. Norma's face can be seen in the porthole window on the other side of the pantry's swinging door. She looks around the kitchen, then opens the door and steps inside. Holly stands nearby, working in the pantry area.

NORMA *(Holding the door, half in and half out of the kitchen)*
Sweetheart, I loved your script. I thought it was so clever.

HOLLY *(Turning to Norma, smiling, and holding a glass of wine)*
Well, you're my mother. Not everybody's gonna be such a sucker.

NORMA *(Gesturing)* I particularly liked the character of the mother. Just a boozy old flirt with a filthy mouth.
Holly chuckles.

NORMA I'm so proud!

HOLLY Oh, Mom, thanks.
Norma steps back out of the kitchen, the door swinging shut behind her. Holly looks at the door, sipping her wine, as the movie cuts back to Hannah's living room. A chubby, friendly uncle sits on a sofa, one child on his lap and several others gathered cross-legged around him on the floor. They lean on the coffee table, which is covered with glasses and a bowl of chips. Other guests mingle in the background; one couple enters the living room, smiling at the scene on the sofa. Mavis crosses the well-lit foyer in the background and opens the door to more guests. The piano plays on.

UNCLE *(Raising his bottle of beer to the children)* Now here's a toast to Thanksgiving, all right?
The children mutter their enthusiastic agreement, picking up their "illicit" glasses of beer.

UNCLE Are we supposed to have beer? Yeeeah!
The uncle pours more beer from his bottle into the kids' outstretched glasses. They cry indistinctly with excitement.

UNCLE *(Overlapping the children's squeals of delight)* Let me at it!
(To one of the little boys) How's that, Fletcher?
Laughing, he turns to the little girl sitting on his lap; he clinks his bottle against the bottle she is holding, which is almost as big as she is.

UNCLE *(To the little girl)*   Doll? To Thanksgiving. Here's a little toast, doll. *(Clinking glasses)* Come on. Bottoms up.
The uncle and the children happily drink their beer as the movie cuts to a wall with subtly patterned wallpaper in Hannah's bedroom. Her face moves on to the screen.

HANNAH *(To an offscreen Elliot)*   Have you been talking to Holly or Lee about us? About our-our personal life?

ELLIOT *(Offscreen)*   Me? Of course not.

HANNAH   There's things Holly wrote about in her script about us that are so . . . personal they could only have come from you.

ELLIOT *(Offscreen)*   Look, I've got a splitting headache and I don't like being accused.
Hannah walks towards Elliot; he's in the bathroom standing over the sink.

HANNAH *(Gesturing)*   I'm not accusing. I'm asking. Do you . . . do you find me too . . . too giving? *(Closing the door of the bathroom slightly so only she is seen on the screen)* Too-too-too competent? Too-too, I don't know, disgustingly perfect or something?

ELLIOT   No.
Elliot walks from behind the partially closed door to an onscreen medicine cabinet.

HANNAH *(Following Elliot and gesturing, talking to his back)*   Well, what is it then? What? Eh, what's come between us? How have I alienated you?

ELLIOT *(Taking a bottle of aspirin from the cabinet and walking back to the sink, gesturing)*   Hannah, my head is throbbing.

HANNAH *(Gesturing)*   You never want to talk about it. I— Every time I bring it up, you-you change the subject. What is it? Do

you— We're communicating less and less. You sleep with me
less and less.

ELLIOT *(Angrily turning to Hannah and pointing as she shouts)*   Hannah, I am very mixed up! Now please!
*Elliot turns back to the sink, once again obscured by the partially
closed door.*

HANNAH *(Reacting, her voice trembling slightly, and gesturing)*   Do
you talk to Holly or Lee behind my back? Do you? You must.
They-they seem to know so much about us.

ELLIOT *(Walking towards a towel rack and gesturing)*   Well, maybe
I've asked advice once or twice or-or made a joke.
He dries his hands as Hannah, standing behind him, continues to talk.

HANNAH *(Gesturing)*   Well, what do you do? Do-do-do you talk
to Holly, or Lee, or what? Do you, do you, do you phone
them?

ELLIOT *(Whirling around to face Hannah, snapping)* Leave me alone, can you?!
He closes the door, briefly obscuring Hannah and himself from view.

ELLIOT *(Continuing in a lower tone)* Jesus, I've told you. I need someone I can matter to.
The camera moves behind the closed door, into the bathroom.

HANNAH *(Reacting, near tears)* You matter to me. Completely.

ELLIOT *(Pausing, his voice rising again)* It's hard to be around someone who gives so much and-and needs so little in return!
He opens the medicine cabinet and puts the aspirin bottle back.

HANNAH *(Gesturing, pleading)* But, look . . . I-I have enormous needs.
Elliot slams the medicine cabinet shut.

ELLIOT *(Shouting)* Well, I can't see them, and neither can Lee or Holly!
He leaves. Hannah watches him go, reacting. She is stunned.

CUT TO:
INTERIOR. HANNAH'S LIVING ROOM — ANOTHER NIGHT.

The dark hallway is illuminated by light coming from the offscreen foyer; pictures line the wall. Piano music is still heard very softly in the background as Hannah, hugging herself, walks slowly down the hallway into the living room. She briefly looks around, lost in thought. She sits down heavily, tiredly, on the arm of the couch as the movie cuts to several framed photographs on the mantel. One shows Hannah and Elliot on their wedding day. Another shows Elliot, obscured in the shadows. Yet another has captured Norma as a young girl. The camera, however, moves closer and closer to a photograph showing Hannah, Lee, and Holly, the three sisters, smiling into the camera. There is no sound.

CUT TO:
INTERIOR. HANNAH'S BEDROOM—NIGHT.

The film shows the bedroom night table, holding a small lamp, a wooden box, a cast-iron fire truck, an ashtray, and glasses. Elliot's pajama-clad arm moves into view. He turns off the lamp; the room is now pitch-black.

HANNAH *(Offscreen)*   It's so pitch-black tonight. I feel lost.

ELLIOT *(Offscreen)*   You're not lost.
Elliot turns the lamp back on, then turns to Hannah; she is lying on her side of the bed, partially in shadow. He leans over and kisses her.

ELLIOT   I love you so much.
They begin to kiss passionately as "Bewitched" starts to play in the background.

CUT TO:

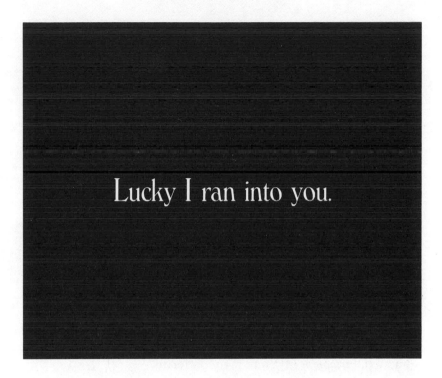

Lucky I ran into you.

"Bewitched" continues as the film cuts to a busy nighttime New York City street. Mickey, his hands in his pockets, walks along the sidewalk, one person among many other pedestrians. He pulls his coat tighter around him as he walks. "Bewitched" continues to play as he passes Tower Records' neon-lit window. He glances inside . . . and sees Holly, her jacket flung over her shoulders, looking at some records.

Mickey walks through the revolving doors of Tower Records, up a few stairs to the selling floor proper, and stops right in front of Holly.

MICKEY *(Gesturing)*   Mmm, I don't know if you remember me, but we had the worst night of my life together.

HOLLY *(Laughing, holding some records)*   I remember you.

MICKEY *(Overlapping)*   Yes, you do recall, right?

HOLLY *(Overlapping, smiling and nodding)*   I recall you.

MICKEY *(Gesturing)*   I was walking past and I saw you in here . . .

HOLLY *(Overlapping, nodding)*   Yeah.

MICKEY   . . . and I thought I'd come in and . . . and we could replay, uh, the whole, uh . . .

HOLLY *(Interrupting, laughing and shaking her head)*   We didn't hit it off.

MICKEY *(Overlapping, smiling)*   Oh, that's putting it mildly. We did everything but exchange gunshots.

HOLLY   How are you?

MICKEY   Good. How are you?

HOLLY   I'm fine.

MICKEY *(Overlapping)*   You look wonderful.

HOLLY *(Chuckling, shaking her head)*   Oh, no.

MICKEY *(Overlapping, scratching his head)*   Yeah, really. You do. You do.

HOLLY   Yeah?

MICKEY   It was a terrible evening.

HOLLY   Yeah, it was.

MICKEY *(Overlapping, gesturing)*   Remember slamming the cab door in my face and . . . *(Touching his nose as Holly laughs)* you know, it came very dangerously close to emasculating my nose in a . . . *(Touching his nose again)*

HOLLY *(Overlapping, laughing)*   I'd never do that.

MICKEY *(Continuing)* . . . in a really horrible way.

HOLLY *(Smiling, glancing away for a moment)* Oh, well, that was a long time ago.

MICKEY *(Overlapping)* You look wonderful. You do. What happened to you?

HOLLY *(Shrugging)* People change . . . you know.

MICKEY *(Touching Holly's shoulder)* Well, I hope you've changed.

HOLLY Yeah, I hope you have, too.

MICKEY *(Overlapping)* I hope so for your sake, because, uh, your personality left something to be desired . . .

HOLLY *(Overlapping, shaking her head)* Yeah, and for yours. I'm sure you've changed.

MICKEY *(Continuing)* . . . namely a personality.
Holly chuckles and turns to look at more records. She walks down the aisle, occasionally glancing at the bins of records. Mickey walks beside her.

MICKEY So how are you?

HOLLY *(Smiling)* I'm okay.

MICKEY You didn't answer my question. What are you doing?

HOLLY Oh, nothing much. You know . . .

MICKEY *(Interrupting)* Well . . .

HOLLY *(Overlapping)* . . . just some stuff. A little of this, a little of that, that's all.

MICKEY *(Overlapping)* Yeah? Is that an embarrassing question? Should I have not asked it?

HOLLY *(Laughing)* Probably not.

MICKEY   Are you, are you out of work or something?

HOLLY   No, well . . . I've been trying to write.

MICKEY   Have you?

HOLLY *(Picking up a record and looking at it)*   Yeah.

MICKEY   Well, that's interesting. Wh-what kind of stuff?

HOLLY *(Touching her chin for a moment)*   Oh . . . well, you-you're not interested in this.

MICKEY *(Overlapping)*   No, you can tell me.

HOLLY   Come on.

MICKEY   No, I am. I am.

HOLLY *(Overlapping)*   Oh, no, millions of people come up to you and say, "Hey, I have something I just wrote," right?

MICKEY   Nobody ever said it.

HOLLY   Really?

MICKEY *(Overlapping)*   This is it. Yeah. This is really—

HOLLY *(Interrupting, turning from the record bins to look at Mickey)*   Well, wo-would you be willing to-to read it? Something . . . that I wrote?

MICKEY *(Nodding his head)*   Well, yes, I would if, uh, if it would mean anything to you. I don't know why it would.

HOLLY *(Laughing, touching her face)*   No, the reason I ask is—

MICKEY *(Overlapping)*   You've always hated my taste in the past.

HOLLY *(Pulling her jacket off her shoulders)*   No, I haven't.

MICKEY   You have.

HOLLY *(Gesturing, looking at Mickey)* I haven't. No, the reason why I ask is I think it might make a great, uh, television script, and, you know, you're so active in television, so—

MICKEY *(Chuckling, gesturing)* I'm not anymore. I haven't, I haven't been in television for a year.

HOLLY You're kidding me.

MICKEY *(Overlapping)* I've done no television whatsoever. No. *As Mickey continues to speak, Holly walks to another bin of records, reacting to his words. She looks offscreen at him, then down at some records. The camera follows her.*

MICKEY *(Offscreen, continuing)* I may, I may have to get back into it, 'cause my accountant says that I'm running out of dollars. But . . . but, um, no, I haven't, I just sort of dropped out for a year . . .

HOLLY *(Overlapping, nodding)* Oh. Oh.

MICKEY *(Offscreen, overlapping)* . . . which is a long, dull story and I won't get into it. But—
Mickey walks back onscreen to Holly. The two of them are partially obscured by a large white Jazz sign imprinted with a large red circle as they continue their conversation.

HOLLY *(Interrupting)* You're okay, though, huh?

MICKEY I'm— Yes. Yes, I'm fine. I'm fine. How are you?

HOLLY *(Face offscreen, obscured by the sign)* Oh, I'm fine.

MICKEY What . . . what about your script? *(Face offscreen, obscured by the sign)* So what's it about?

HOLLY *(Face offscreen)* Well, I'd love it if you'd read it, actually, 'cause I really would value your opinion.

MICKEY *(Face offscreen)* You have to remember, we-we-we didn't agree on one thing.
They emerge from behind the Jazz sign, still walking, still talking.

HOLLY *(Smiling, gesturing)* But you have to remember while you're reading and you're cursing my name, you know, that this is my first script. Well, it's not my first script.

MICKEY Hmm.

HOLLY *(Touching her face)* Actually, my first script was about Hannah and her husband, but, uh . . .

MICKEY Yeah?

HOLLY . . . Hannah read it, she got really angry, and . . . you know, then I felt badly, so I—
She picks up a record.

MICKEY *(Overlapping)* Oh, well, God, I can imagine what you wrote.

HOLLY Oh, no! It wasn't anything bad. But she just . . . you know. I don't know.
Mickey pulls out a record and looks at it.

MICKEY Really?

HOLLY So, uh . . . I threw it out, but I have this other one.
Holly looks hopefully at Mickey.

MICKEY Well, you know, I-I-I . . . you know, if you want me to, I'll read it.

HOLLY *(Overlapping, gesturing)* Oh, gosh, I don't know. *(Pausing)* Well, could I come over tomorrow and read it to you?

MICKEY *(Chuckling)* Come over tomorrow and read it to me?
Holly laughs, embarrassed, as Mickey puts the record he's been looking at back in the bin.

MICKEY   You must be joking. I've been doing all my own reading since I was forty . . . you know.

HOLLY *(Laughing, looking at Mickey)*   Hmm. I think it's lucky I
ran into you. *(Laughing)* Maybe.

MICKEY *(Laughing)*   Well, what about me?

HOLLY *(Chuckling, waving her arm)*   Oh, well.

MICKEY *(Overlapping, gesturing)*   I should have kept going. I-I
have a sneaking feeling, a nagging sensation I should've kept
walking and . . .
Holly chuckles, looking off for a moment.

MICKEY *(Continuing, looking at Holly)*   . . . and not begun this
conversation.
There is a brief pause and the movie cuts to:

INTERIOR. MICKEY'S APARTMENT—DAY.

*The screen shows a chaise in Mickey's apartment; an ashtray on a
stand sits nearby. The camera moves down the chaise, past several
piles of books, to Mickey's coffee table. He sits, picking at his fingers
and listening, on the edge of the table in front of Holly, who is sitting
cross-legged on the floor, propped up with a pillow, reading her script
aloud.*

HOLLY *(Offscreen, as the camera moves across the room towards her and
Mickey, reading)*   "We all go through life playing the hand
we're dealt. Craig: And what hand were you dealt?" *(Onscreen
now)* "Emily: I'm two high pair, maybe even aces up. The
problem is, you've got three deuces."
Holly closes the script and looks up at Mickey.

HOLLY   That's the end.
Mickey smiles and shrugs, not knowing what to say.

HOLLY   No, you can tell me straight. It's okay. Just, you know, tell me what you think.

MICKEY *(Shaking his head, shrugging)*   It's great. I swea— I'm— I'm, tch, I'm speechless. I was . . . I was not in the mood to listen to this thing now. *(Sighing)* I don't know what to say. I'm moved and I laughed and I— Uh, I, you know, I was on the edge of my seat. I just think it's wonderful! I'm, I'm totally . . . stunned. This is not an insult. I'm amazed that you can . . . *(Sighing)* It was— I just thought it was great.

HOLLY *(Reacting)*   Really?

MICKEY *(Grunting and gesturing)*   Yes! I was abso— And . . . w-what . . . made you think of that climax scene where the, where the . . . architect is walking home with his actress girl-friend and-and the ex-wife who's schizophrenic jumps out of the bushes and stabs him to death?

HOLLY *(Laughing and nodding)*   Oh, it just came to me one day.

MICKEY *(Gesturing)*   Well, it was just fabulous! I'm, I, you know . . .

HOLLY *(Gasping, hitting her forehead with her hand)*   Oh, gosh, you really think I can write?

MICKEY *(Gesturing)*   I thought it was wonder— There's maybe one or two things in there that I would do differently myself, but . . .

HOLLY *(Gasping and nodding)*   Right.

MICKEY *(Continuing)*   . . . but who cares? It was just— *(Gesturing)* It was fabulous.

HOLLY *(Chuckling)*   Oh!

HANNAH AND HER SISTERS

MICKEY *(Smiling and shaking his head)*   Fabulous, I mean it! I'm so impressed.

Holly, thrilled with Mickey's overwhelming response, stands up, her hand on her head. Unable to contain herself, she begins to walk up and down the room, holding her script. The camera follows her; Mickey is now offscreen.

HOLLY *(Laughing)*   Oh, God!

MICKEY *(Offscreen, overlapping)*   I am. You-you made my day.

HOLLY *(Gasping)*   Oh, wow!

MICKEY *(Offscreen)*   It was just great. Uh, I was all set . . . I was set to be bored stiff.

HOLLY *(Grinning, looking at the offscreen Mickey)*   Uh, gee. Would you like to have lunch? Uh, uh . . .

MICKEY *(Offscreen)*   I-I would love to talk to you about, uh, that script. I-I, you know, I think maybe that we could do something with it.

HOLLY *(Nodding)*   Okay, and listen, I would like to hear what made you suddenly decide to drop out of life.

MICKEY *(Offscreen)*   Oh, who cares?

HOLLY *(Gesturing)*   Y-you used to— Oh, no! Yeah, I care. You used to be so ambitious and . . . *(Pausing, grinning)* God, you really liked it?!
"You Made Me Love You" starts to play as the movie cuts to the street outside Mickey's apartment house, an old building complete with a red entrance door and a gray, weather-beaten façade. Trees line the sidewalk. Holly and Mickey emerge from the door and walk up the street, revealing a whole row of similar apartment buildings. They pass a few other people as they walk.

The film then moves to the outside of a charming glass and stained-wood café. Through the window, Holly and Mickey can be seen having lunch. Holly is talking animatedly; Mickey takes a sip of coffee. Some people pass by.

Next, the film cuts to an almost isolated path in Central Park, complete with old-fashioned streetlamps and scattered leaves. Holly and Mickey stroll into view, deep in conversation.

HOLLY *(Gesturing)*   Gosh, you really went through a crisis, you know that? H-how did you get over it? I mean, when I ran into you, you seemed, you seemed just perfectly fine. Well, you seem fine now.

MICKEY   Well . . . *(Chuckling)* I'll tell you. *(Sighing)* One day about a month ago . . .
The film abruptly cuts to Mickey's flashback, a visual counterpoint to the story he is telling Holly. A close-up of a nervous, perspiring, and panting Mickey alone in his apartment appears on the screen as his voice is heard.

HANNAH AND HER SISTERS

MICKEY'S VOICE-OVER . . . I really hit bottom. You know, I just felt that in a Godless universe, I didn't want to go on living. Now I happen to own this rifle . . . *(Coughing)*
Mickey raises the barrel of a rifle to his forehead. He shuts his eyes tightly.

MICKEY'S VOICE-OVER . . . which I loaded, believe it or not, and pressed it to my forehead. And I remember thinking, at the time, I'm gonna kill myself. Then I thought . . . what if I'm wrong? What if there is a God? I mean, after all, nobody really knows that.
The camera moves past the desperate Mickey to a mirror on the wall behind him. Its reflection shows his spiral staircase and some standing lamps. A clock faintly ticks.

MICKEY'S VOICE-OVER But then I thought, no. You know, maybe is not good enough. I want certainty or nothing. And I remember very clearly the clock was ticking, and I was sitting there frozen, with the gun to my head, debating whether to shoot.
The gun goes off with a loud bang. The mirror shatters.

MICKEY'S VOICE-OVER All of a sudden, the gun went off.
Mickey, holding the rifle, is seen running over to the shattered mirror. The sounds of his excited neighbors, their shouting, a knocking door, are heard as he continues his tale.

MICKEY'S VOICE-OVER I had been so tense, my finger had squeezed the trigger inadvertently . . .

NEIGHBOR #1 *(Offscreen, overlapping)* What's happening? Wh-wh-what's going on?

MICKEY'S VOICE-OVER *(Continuing)* . . . but I was perspiring so much, the gun had slid off my forehead and missed me.

NEIGHBOR #2 *(Offscreen, overlapping)* I don't know. I heard a gun. Is everything all right?
Mickey, still brandishing the rifle, runs into his sunlit living room. He looks around frantically, his shirt loose. Finally, he throws the rifle down between the sofa and the coffee table. The gun goes off a second time. Mickey, standing nearby, jumps, his hands flying to his head. The doorbell rings; the neighbors begin pounding at the door.

MICKEY'S VOICE-OVER And suddenly, neighbors were, were, pounding on the door, and-and I don't know, the whole scene was just pandemonium. And, uh, you know, and I-I-I-I-I ran to the door.
Mickey runs offscreen briefly to answer the door.

MICKEY'S VOICE-OVER I-I-I-I didn't know what to say. You know, I was, I was embarrassed and confused, and my-my-my mind was r-r-racing a mile a minute . . .
He returns onscreen, panting; he looks frantically once again around the living room.

MICKEY'S VOICE-OVER . . . and I-I just knew one thing.
The film cuts to a West Side street. It's an overcast day. Mickey, walking slowly along the sidewalk, passes several other pedestrians and numerous storefronts, including Klein's Pharmacy and a "Bar-B-Q" take-out. Occasionally, he is obscured by a tree trunk on the opposite side of the street; a few taxis go by as he talks over the scene.

MICKEY'S VOICE-OVER I . . . I-I-I-I had to get out of that house. I had to just get out in the fresh air and-and clear my head. And I remember very clearly, I walked the streets. I walked and I walked. I-I didn't know what was going through my mind. It all seemed so violent and un-unreal to me. And I wandered . . .
The movie cuts to the exterior of the Metro movie theater, with its smoked glass entrance doors and its Art Deco feel. An old publicity photo hangs inside. Mickey's reflection is seen at the almost-transparent

doors, as well as the reflection of the street and various cars whizzing by. His reflection walks towards the theater entrance; he continues his story.

MICKEY'S VOICE-OVER . . . for a long time on the Upper West Side, you know, an-and it must have been hours! You know, my, my feet hurt. My head was, was pounding, and, and I had to sit down. I went into a movie house. I-I didn't know what was playing or anything.
Mickey walks into the movie house. He is seen through the glass doors, which still reflect the street and traffic outside. He makes his way through the lobby into the actual theater.

MICKEY'S VOICE-OVER I just, I just needed a moment to gather my thoughts and, and be logical, and, and put the world back into rational perspective.
The film abruptly cuts to the theater's black-and-white screen, where the Marx Brothers, in Duck Soup, *play the helmets of several soldiers standing in a line like a live xylophone. The sounds of the "xylophone" are heard as the movie cuts to the darkened theater, where Mickey slowly sits down in a balcony seat. The "xylophone" music stops and changes to "Hidee-hidee-hidee-hidee-hidee-hidee-ho" as sung by the Marx Brothers and ensemble in the movie. The singing continues faintly in the background as Mickey continues his tale:*

MICKEY'S VOICE-OVER And I went upstairs to the balcony, and I sat down *(Sighing)* and, you know, the movie was a-a-a film that I'd seen many times in my life since I was a kid, an-and I always u-uh, loved it. And, you know, I'm, I'm watching these people up on the screen, and I started getting hooked o-on the film, you know?
The film cuts back to the black-and-white movie screen as Mickey continues to talk. The Marx Brothers, as well as the hundred-odd other cast members in Duck Soup, *are kneeling and bowing as they sing "Hidee-hidee-ho." They kick their heels up in the air. They sway back and forth, hands clasped, singing "Oh-h-h-h-h-h . . ."*

MICKEY'S VOICE-OVER   . . . And I started to feel how can you even think of killing yourself? I mean, isn't it so stupid? I mean, l-look at all the people up there on the screen. You know, they're real funny, and, and what if the worst *is* true?
The movie cuts back to Mickey, sitting almost obscured in the dark theater. The Oh-h-h-h-h-h's coming from the offscreen movie are heard as he continues to speak.

MICKEY'S VOICE-OVER   What if there's no God, and you only go around once and that's it? Well, you know, don't you want to be part of the experience? You know, what the hell, it-i-it's not *all* a drag. And I'm thinking to myself, geez, I should stop ruining my life . . .
As Mickey talks, the film cuts back to the antics of the Marx Brothers on the black-and-white theater screen. The four brothers are now swaying and singing and strutting, their voices indistinct over Mickey's narration.

MICKEY'S VOICE-OVER   . . . searching for answers I'm never gonna get, and just enjoy it while it lasts. And . . . you know . . .
The film is back on Mickey's dark form in the audience.

MICKEY'S VOICE-OVER   . . . after, who knows? I mean, you know, maybe there is something. Nobody really knows. I know, I know "maybe" is a very slim reed to hang your whole life on, but that's the best we have. And . . . then, I started to sit back, and I actually began to enjoy myself.
As Mickey continues, the film cuts back to Duck Soup *on the black-and-white screen. The Marx Brothers are sitting on a judge's bench, playing banjos and singing with the other cast members. They jump down from the bench, still singing. Their voices swell.*

MARX BROTHERS & COMPANY   "Oh, Freedonia / Oh, don't you cry for me / They'll be coming around the mountain . . ."
The Marx Brothers kneel, strumming their banjos, and the movie cuts

back to Central Park. The flashback is over. Mickey and Holly con-
tinue their stroll as "You Made Me Love You" begins to play in the
background. They pass some people, a cluster of buildings that look
like castles, and the Manhattan skyline as seen through the trees, as
the camera moves back, farther and farther away from them, showing
a beautiful Central Park, frozen in time.

HOLLY *(Gesturing)* Um . . . look, there's something I've, uh, that's been bothering me for a long time, and I just thought I'd just tell you what it was and just sort of clear the deck here, and *(Chuckling)* that's this.

MICKEY *(Mumbling)* Oh, yeah? What?

HOLLY *(Overlapping)* That I've always regretted the way I behaved that evening we went out, and, uh . . . I've, I just thought I'd tell you that because I really made a fool out of myself.

MICKEY Oh, don't be silly! No! Don't be ridiculous.

HOLLY *(Overlapping)* It's all right.

MICKEY I was the, I was . . . You know, it was my fault. I—
(Inhaling)
Holly laughs.

MICKEY So, so you want to go out to dinner again? I mean, is that, is that . . . Have, you have any interest in that, or . . .

HOLLY Sure. Sure, uh, yes.

MICKEY *(Overlapping)* Do you? I mean, are you, are you, are you, are you free this evening?

HOLLY Yeah.
They stroll offscreen. "You Made Me Love You" grows louder and the
film cuts to:

One year later.

CUT TO:
INTERIOR. HANNAH'S APARTMENT—THANKSGIVING NIGHT.

A large, perfectly roasted turkey on a serving plate briefly fills the screen as the camera moves across the food-laden table in Hannah's kitchen, past an electric mixer, several bowls, spices, tomatoes, and parsley, to reveal Evan walking through the doorway.

EVAN *(Holding a drink)*   I want ice! Who's got some— *(Pointing to an ice bucket on the table)* Oh, there it is.

HANNAH *(Offscreen, overlapping)*   It's on the table, Dad.
The sounds of Thanksgiving guests in the other rooms are dimly heard; "You Made Me Love You" continues softly in the background. Mavis passes the table, licking some food off her hand. Hannah, in the background, is busy by the stove.

EVAN *(Putting ice into his glass)*   Hey, where's Holly? She's late.
As Mavis leaves the kitchen, Lee enters, carrying some empty glasses.

LEE *(Walking briskly to the sink)*   Hey, Hannah, did you read that
last thing Holly wrote? It was great. She's really developed.

HANNAH *(Offscreen, in another area of the kitchen)*   I know, she . . .
she really writes good dialogue.

LEE *(Turning to the offscreen Hannah)*   Yeah. I'll get some ice.
*Lee walks off, drying her wet hands in the air. Hannah, in a silk
dress, moves onscreen, going to the table and pouring herself a glass of
wine as Norma enters the kitchen.*

NORMA   Hannah, can I tell everybody you're going to play Des-
demona?
*Norma walks over to a glass-doored cabinet and takes out a bottle of
gin.*

HANNAH *(Taking a big sip of her wine)*   Oh, Mom, it's only television. *(Beginning to mash some sweet potatoes in a bowl on the
table)*

NORMA *(Gesturing with the bottle)*   Yes, but it's public television.
And to me, Shakespeare doesn't get any greater than *Othello*.
You with some big black stud! I love it!
*Norma unscrews the liquor bottle and pours some into her empty glass
as Hannah stops her mashing, reacting.*

HANNAH *(Gasping and laughing)*   Oh, Mom!

EVAN *(Overlapping, reacting)*   Oh, honey!
*The movie leaves the kitchen and cuts to the doorway between the
dining room and the living room. Upbeat jazz plays over the low din
of the party. Two women stand by the partially set dining room table,
chatting and arranging some plates, as Elliot strolls into view, sipping
a drink. He passes the women and walks through the doorway into the
living room, nodding hello to a guest who is walking the other way.*

He enters the living room, smiling. It is crowded with guests; Hannah's children play in their midst. One of Hannah's boys grabs Elliot's arm. They playfully "spar" for a moment before Elliot laughingly shakes him off, continuing on his way into a connecting room. He stops at the doorway, looking at the crowd. The camera shows his point of view: Guests stand in clusters, enjoying themselves; one woman chats with a little boy; another woman, carrying a drink, walks over to a group of other guests.

The film then cuts back briefly to Elliot, holding his drink and looking straight ahead, as it shows his point of view once more. This time he sees a smiling Lee and Doug, talking animatedly; a few guests are seen in the background. Elliot's voice is heard over a close-up of the couple.

ELLIOT'S VOICE-OVER   Oh, Lee, you are something.
Lee and Doug kiss each other. They continue talking.

ELLIOT'S VOICE-OVER   You look very beautiful. Marriage agrees with you. Everything that happened between us *(Pausing)* seems more and more hazy.
As Lee takes a sip of her drink, the movie cuts back to Elliot, standing in the doorway and still staring straight ahead. The camera moves in closer to his face as he talks over the scene.

ELLIOT'S VOICE-OVER   I acted like such a fool. I don't know what came over me. The complete conviction that I couldn't live without you.
The film quickly cuts to a brief look at Lee and Doug, still talking animatedly and smiling. Lee gently pushes back Doug's hair.

ELLIOT'S VOICE-OVER   What did I put us both through? And Hannah . . .
The camera moves back to Elliot.

ELLIOT'S VOICE-OVER *(Continuing)*   . . . who as you once said, I love much more than I realized.

After pausing for a moment on Elliot's face, the film cuts to the foyer, where two boys and a girl gather by the door. One boy opens it, revealing Holly. She joyfully enters the apartment, greeting each child with an enthusiastic kiss.

HOLLY *(Kissing the children)* Hi! How are you! *(Kissing)* Happy Thanksgiving! *(Kissing)*

BOY #1 Hi!

HOLLY I didn't miss dinner, did I?

THE CHILDREN *(Overlapping, talking at once)* No!
The jazz ends as the record scratches and stops. Evan's rendition of "Isn't It Romantic" is heard on the piano as Holly, shrugging the strap of her pocketbook off her shoulder, walks towards the living room. She is stopped by three guests—two women, one of them wearing glasses, and a man—who are coming out of the room.

HOLLY *(Smiling)* Huh? Hi, Marge.

FEMALE GUEST #1 *(Overlapping)*   You look lovely.
They kiss.

FEMALE GUEST #2 *(Overlapping, hugging Holly)*   Hello, darling.

HOLLY   Happy Thanksgiving.

FEMALE GUEST #2 *(Overlapping)*   Good to see you. Same to you.

HOLLY *(Hugging the man)*   Hello.
The movie cuts to Hannah, leaning contentedly against a doorway into the living room and listening to the offscreen Evan play the piano. Elliot, holding his drink, walks over to her. They look at each other for a beat; Elliot then hugs Hannah, pulling her towards him. She leans her head on his shoulder, fingering his jacket lapel. They look offscreen together, happily, intimately, at the offscreen guests, as the camera moves across the room, past a few guests, to reveal Evan sitting at the piano. Norma sits at his side, one arm resting on the piano. She holds a drink and looks off in the distance, mouthing the words to "Isn't It Romantic."

The camera then moves to the doorway in the living room, where a man, holding a drink, enters and joins the happy crowd. Evan can be seen in the background, playing his song. A child plays near the coffee table.

The camera continues to move past the doorway, past a huge grand-father clock, to a second doorway leading to the den. Here, more guests are gathered; a child sits in a small chair by the sofa. He sips a soda as female guest #2 enters the room and crouches down next to him, smiling. She waves to him. He waves back as the camera continues to move past the doorway to reveal Holly, standing in front of a hallway mirror, fixing her earrings. Mavis can be seen in the background, through the doorway into the dining room, lighting the candles on the table. She dims the lights, darkening the room and the hallway where Holly stands in a warm candlelit glow. Mavis leaves the dining room and passes Holly.

HOLLY *(Still fixing her earrings, to Mavis)*   It's beautiful.
Mavis walks off. Holly, reflected in the mirror, begins fluffing her hair as Mickey enters and wraps his arms around her from behind. The camera stays focused on the mirror; both Holly and Mickey are now seen in its reflection.

MICKEY *(Smacking his lips)*   Now don't get nervous. It's just your husband.

HOLLY *(Grinning)*   Hi.

MICKEY   Hi. *(Kissing Holly)*   How you doin'?

HOLLY *(Nestling against Mickey)*   Okay.

MICKEY   When'd you get here?

HOLLY   Just a few minutes ago.

MICKEY   Oh. *(Kissing her again)*   You look so beautiful.

Mickey continues to kiss Holly. She responds, sighing and closing her eyes.

HOLLY Thanks.

MICKEY *(Kissing Holly's neck)* You know, I was talking with your father before . . . and I was telling him that *(Kissing)* it's ironic. I-I used to always have Thanksgiving with Hannah . . . and I never thought *(Kissing)* that I could love anybody else. *(Kissing)* And here it is, years later and I'm married to you *(Kissing)* and completely in love with you. *(Kissing)* The heart is a very, very resilient little muscle. *(Kissing)* It really is. I . . . *(Kissing)* It'd make a great story, I think. A guy marries one sister . . . *(Kissing)* doesn't work out . . . *(Kissing)* many years later . . . *(Kissing)* he winds up *(Inhaling)* married to the other sister. It's, you know, it's a . . .

HOLLY *(Fondling Mickey's arm, smiling)* Tch.

MICKEY *(Overlapping)*   I don't know how you're gonna top that.
Mickey continues to kiss Holly's neck; he chuckles.

HOLLY *(Kissing Mickey's cheek)*   Mickey?

MICKEY *(Kissing Holly's neck)*   Mmm, what?

HOLLY   I'm pregnant.
The mirror shows Mickey pulling away slightly, reacting. They look at each other at arm's length, Holly grinning, Mickey in shock, then embrace and kiss passionately, tighter and tighter, as the music swells . . .

And the credits appear, white on a black screen:

WITH

JULIE KAVNER

BOBBY SHORT

JOANNA GLEASON

ASSOCIATE PRODUCER

GAIL SICILIA

PRODUCTION MANAGER

EZRA SWERDLOW

FIRST ASSISTANT DIRECTOR

THOMAS REILLY

SECOND ASSISTANT DIRECTOR

KEN ORNSTEIN

Production Coordinator	HELEN ROBIN
Script Supervisor	KAY CHAPIN
Assistant to Mr. Allen	JANE READ MARTIN
Production Auditor	JOSEPH HARTWICK
Set Decorator	CAROL JOFFE
Set Dresser	DAVE WEINMAN
Property Master	JAMES MAZZOLA
Standby Scenic Artist	JAMES SORICE
Camera Operator	DICK MINGALONE
Assistant Cameraman	DOUGLAS C. HART

Second Assistant Cameraman	BOB PAONE
Still Photographer	BRIAN HAMILL
Additional Photography	JAMIE JACOBSEN
Production Sound Mixer	LES LAZAROWITZ
Boom Operator	LINDA MURPHY
Sound Recordist	TOD MAITLAND
Re-recording Mixer	LEE DICHTER
	SOUND ONE CORP.
Key Grip	BOB WARD
Dolly Grip	RONALD BURKE
Gaffer	RAY QUINLAN
Best Boy	VIN DELANEY
Make-up Design	FERN BUCHNER
Hair Design	ROMAINE GREENE
Men's Wardrobe Supervisor	MARK BURCHARD
Women's Wardrobe Supervisor	PATRICIA EIBEN
Associate to Mr. Kurland	TOM MCKINLEY

"Isn't It Romantic" ends. Uptempo jazz begins playing for the remainder of the credits on the screen.

Location Manager	TIMOTHY MARSHALL BOURNE
Location Coordinator	SANDY NELSON
Location Scouts	DANA ROBIN
	NICHOLAS BERNSTEIN
	BARBARA HELLER
	ORA RAMAT
Assistant Production Coordinator	AMY HERMAN
DGA Trainee	SALLY ANDREWS
Production Staff	KRIS COLE
	JAMES DAVIS
	PAM GARTRELL
	HILLARY ROLLINS
	ANGELA SALGADO
	JUD SCHWARTZ
Casting Assistant	ELLEN LEWIS
Additional Casting	TODD MICHAEL THALER
Transportation Captain	HARRY LEAVEY

HANNAH AND HER SISTERS

Assistant Production Auditor	RICHARD GUAY
Assistant to Mr. Wurtzel	DAN LEIGH
Projectionist	CARL TURNQUEST, JR.
Assistant Film Editors	RICHARD NORD
	SUZANNE PILLSBURY
Sound Editor	JACK FITZSTEPHENS
Assistant Sound Editor	NOREEN EVANS
Apprentice Film Editor	NICOLE HOLOFCENER
Color by	TECHNICOLOR®
Prints by	DELUXE®
Art Cards	COMPUTER OPTICALS
Optical	ASSOCIATES & FERREN
Titles	THE OPTICAL HOUSE, N.Y.

LENSES AND PANAFLEX® CAMERAS BY PANAVISION®

Segment from the opera *Manon Lescaut* by Puccini
Filmed at the Regio Theater of Turin, Italy
The Orchestra of the Regio Theater
Conductor — Angelo Campori
Director — Carlo Maestrini
Sets — Pasquale Grassi
Costumes — Tirelli Costumes, Rome

"You Made Me Love You"
by Joseph McCarthy & James V. Monaco
Performed by Harry James
Courtesy of Capitol Records, Inc.

"I've Heard That Song Before"
by Sammy Cahn & Jule Styne
Performed by Harry James
Courtesy of Capitol Records, Inc.

"Bewitched"
by Richard Rodgers & Lorenz Hart

"Just You, Just Me"
by Raymond Klages & Jesse Greer

WOODY ALLEN

"Where or When"
by Richard Rodgers & Lorenz Hart

"Concerto for Two Violins & Orchestra"
by J. S. Bach
The Sofia Soloists Chamber Orchestra
Conducted by Vassil Kazandjiev
Solo Violins: Georgi Badev & Stoika Milanova
Courtesy of Monitor Records

"Back to the Apple"
by Frank Foster & Count Basie
Performed by Count Basie & His Orchestra
Courtesy of Roulette Records, Inc.

"The Trot"
by Benny Carter
Performed by Count Basie & His Orchestra
Courtesy of Roulette Records, Inc.

"I Remember You"
by Johnny Mercer & Victor Schertzinger
Performed by Dave Brubeck
Courtesy of Fantasy Records

"Madame Butterfly"
by Puccini
Performed by Rome Opera Chorus & Orchestra
Conducted by Sir John Barbirolli
Courtesy of EMI Records, Inc.

"Concerto for Harpsichord in F Minor"
by J. S. Bach
Performed by Leonhardt Gustav
Leonhardt—Consort
Courtesy of Teldec Schallplatten GMBH

"You Are Too Beautiful"
by Richard Rodgers & Lorenz Hart

HANNAH AND HER SISTERS

"If I Had You"
by Jimmy Campbell, Reg Connelly & Ted Shapiro
Performed by Roy Eldridge

"I'm In Love Again"
by Cole Porter

"I'm Old-Fashioned"
by Jerome Kern & Johnny Mercer

"The Way You Look Tonight"
by Jerome Kern & Dorothy Fields

"It Could Happen to You"
by Johnny Burke & James Van Heusen

"Polkadots and Moonbeams"
by Johnny Burke & James Van Heusen

"Avalon"
by Vincent Rose, Al Jolson & B. G. De Sylva

"Isn't It Romantic"
by Richard Rodgers & Lorenz Hart

The Cast
(in order of appearance)

BARBARA HERSHEY	*Lee*
CARRIE FISHER	*April*
MICHAEL CAINE	*Elliot*
MIA FARROW	*Hannah*
DIANNE WIEST	*Holly*
MAUREEN O'SULLIVAN	*Norma*
LLOYD NOLAN	*Evan*
MAX VON SYDOW	*Frederick*
WOODY ALLEN	*Mickey*
LEWIS BLACK	*Paul*
JULIA LOUIS-DREYFUS	*Mary*
CHRISTIAN CLEMENSON	*Larry*

JULIE KAVNER	*Gail*
J. T. WALSH	*Ed Smythe*
JOHN TURTURRO	*Writer*
RUSTY MAGEE	*Ron*
ALLEN DECHESER	*Hannah's Twins*
ARTIE DECHESER	
IRA WHEELER	*Dr. Abel*
RICHARD JENKINS	*Dr. Wilkes*
TRACY KENNEDY	*Brunch Guest*
FRED MELAMED	*Dr. Grey*
BENNO SCHMIDT	*Dr. Smith*
JOANNA GLEASON	*Carol*
MARIA CHIARA	*Manon Lescaut*
DANIEL STERN	*Dusty*
STEPHEN DEFLUITER	*Dr. Brooks*
THE 39 STEPS	*Rock Band*
BOBBY SHORT	*Himself*
ROB SCOTT	*Drummer*
BEVERLY PEER	*Bass Player*
DAISY PREVIN	*Hannah's Children*
MOSES FARROW	
PAUL BATES	*Theater Manager*
CARROTTE	*Theater Executives*
MARY PAPPAS	
BERNIE LEIGHTON	*Audition Pianist*
KEN COSTIGAN	*Father Flynn*
HELEN MILLER	*Mickey's Mother*
LEO POSTREL	*Mickey's Father*
SUSAN GORDON-CLARK	*Hostess*
WILLIAM STURGIS	*Elliot's Analyst*
DANIEL HABER	*Krishna*
VERNA O. HOBSON	*Mavis*
JOHN DOUMANIAN	*Thanksgiving Guests*
FLETCHER PREVIN	
IRWIN TENENBAUM	

AMY GREENHILL
DICKSON SHAW
MARJE SHERIDAN
IVAN KRONENFELD   *Lee's Husband*

The producers gratefully acknowledge and wish to thank the
following for their assistance:

The Mayor's Office of Film, Theatre and Broadcasting
Chappell & Co, Inc.
CBS Robbins Catalogue, Inc.
General Camera Corp.
Lee Lighting America Ltd.
Albert G. Ruben Insurance Co., Inc.
Alta Marea Productions, Inc.
On Location Education, Inc.
Summit Waterproofing & Restoration Corp.
Frederick's Oils courtesy of Marshall Arisman
Frederick's Drawings courtesy of Randall Rupert
The Choir of the Church of The Transfiguration,
John Gordon Morris, Choirmaster

(Emblem)
MOTION PICTURE ASSOCIATION OF AMERICA
Approved No. 27862

An ORION PICTURES Release

ABOUT THE AUTHOR

After he was rejected from both New York University and City College, Woody Allen turned to a professional writing career, at first for television and comedians. In 1964 he decided to become a comedian himself.

Woody Allen's first screenplay, written in 1964, was the enormously popular *What's New, Pussycat?* He has also written, directed, and starred in thirteen films to date: *Take the Money and Run, Bananas, Everything You Always Wanted to Know About Sex, Sleeper, Love and Death, Annie Hall, Manhattan, Stardust Memories, A Midsummer Night's Sex Comedy, Broadway Danny Rose, Zelig, The Purple Rose of Cairo* and *Hannah and Her Sisters.* Mr. Allen also wrote and directed *Interiors.* In addition, Mr. Allen has written three plays for Broadway: *Don't Drink the Water, Play It Again, Sam* (the latter starring himself in both the play and the subsequent film version) and *The Floating Lightbulb.*

Mr. Allen has written and appeared in his own television specials and has been a frequent contributor to *The New Yorker,* among other periodicals.